Stop Hurting the Woman You Love

Stop Hurting the Woman You Love
Breaking the Cycle of Abusive Behavior

Charlie Donaldson, M.A., and Randy Flood, M.A.,
with Elaine Eldridge, Ph.D.

 HAZELDEN®

Hazelden
Center City, Minnesota 55012-0176
1-800-328-0094
1-651-213-4590 (Fax)
www.hazelden.org
© 2006 by Charlie Donaldson, Randy Flood, Elaine Eldridge

Library of Congress Cataloging-in-Publication Data
Donaldson, Charlie, 1945–
    Stop hurting the woman you love : breaking the cycle of
abusive behavior / Charlie Donaldson and Randy Flood,
with Elaine Eldridge.
        p. cm.
    Includes bibliographical references and index.
    ISBN-13: 978-1-59285-354-0
    ISBN-10: 1-59285-354-4
    1. Family violence—United States. 2. Family violence—
United States—Case studies. 3 Family violence—United
States—Prevention. 4. Wife abuse—United States. 5. Wife
abuse—United States—Prevention. I. Flood, Randy, 1963–
II. Eldridge, Elaine, 1951– III. Title.

HV6626.2.D62 2006
616.85'822—dc22

                                                    2005056393

09 08 07 06 05 6 5 4 3 2 1

Cover design by David Spohn
Interior design and typesetting by Stanton Publication Services, Inc.

Contents

Acknowledgments

We cannot begin to acknowledge all the people and organizations that have contributed to our professional development, but we do want to thank the Coordinated Community of Domestic Abuse, the Lakeshore Alliance Against Domestic and Sexual Violence of Ottawa County, and the Domestic Violence Coordinated Community Response Teams of Kent County. We have also benefited from conferences, training, and relationships with other professionals in the field of domestic abuse: Paul Kivel, Jackson Katz, John Lee, Michael S. Kimmel, and Robert Bly have helped us develop our ideas about the state of masculinity in the twenty-first century, and Ellen Pense, Donald Dutton, Jacklyn Campbell, Lundy Bancroft, William Gondolf, and Anne Ganley have broadened and deepened our understanding of the dynamics of domestic abuse.

We also want to acknowledge the men in our domestic abuse treatment groups who have been courageous enough to engage in the difficult work of change. Their experiences and struggles as they reach for accountability have given us the intimate knowledge we needed to write this book with truth and care. We also want to acknowledge the partners of these men. We admire their strength in making difficult decisions about their relationships with abusive men, and we admire their courage to make new lives for themselves and their children.

Melissa Dunham and Becky Plantinga at Fountain Hill Center for Counseling and Consultation assisted in developing cycles and graphs. Brian Distelberg helped us create the "What Kind of Man Am I?" questionnaire by using statistical norming to select questions and to standardize the scoring, and Al Heystek administered the questionnaire to his group members.

Thanks to our readers, Amy VanGunst, Stephanie Flood, and Al Heystek, for their useful edits and suggestions.

Randy Flood

Charlie has been an energetic and disciplined presence in my life, helping me stay focused on this project when life got busy. Elaine joined us as a writer, but she contributed above and beyond in challenging Charlie and me conceptually and theoretically as well as grammatically.

I particularly want to thank Amy VanGunst; her insights on the effects of domestic abuse on women and families have helped me in my work with men. I have also learned from my discussions of difficult cases with Al Heystek and Bev Becksforth and with Kirk Brink and Sally Ryan.

I would like to acknowledge my wife, Stephanie, and our children, Zachary and Anna, who were supportive and patient during the time it took to write this book. These relationships have taught me a lot about intimacy: love, vulnerability, commitment, and emotional involvement.

I thank my parents for showing me that troubled relationships can heal in spite of past pain. My father, Larry, broke the generational cycle of domestic abuse by refusing to stay on his father's path. Because he had the strength and love to change his course in life, I have been able to take the next step of helping other men to develop more loving and respectful relationships with their partners.

Charlie Donaldson

I am grateful to colleagues who have helped me grow as a therapist and deepen my understanding of domestic abuse. In addition to members of the institutions mentioned above, I want to thank the staffs of the 58th District Court and the Center for Women in Transition. I also want to thank Dave Schipper, Ortencia Bos, Jill Vaandering, and the Honorable Susan Jonas, who have served as mentors and standard bearers in the essential work we do. I thank Elaine for her exceptional writing and organizational skills, and for her persistence in seeking excellence. Finally, I am grateful to Randy for ten years of collaboration, for partnering to create the Men's Resource Center and so many other endeavors, and for his humor and perseverance no matter how deep the slough or frightening the torrent.

I also want to announce my daily and heartfelt gratitude to Patricia Genesky, manager of the Men's Resource Center, Holland, who makes all things possible; my colleague Tara Romano, whose depth, clinical skills, and wisdom continually amaze me; the women in my life, Carol, Diane, and Sylvia, and the men in my men's group, all of whom have sometimes taught me more about myself than I wanted to know; my sisters, Kathy and Nancy, my cousin, Linda, and my son, Shawn, who have been so loving and who do such important work of their own; and most importantly, my mother for her love, advice, and encouragement, and for demonstrating the heartiness and courage that I want to flow through all of my life.

Elaine Eldridge

Thanks, first, to Charlie for his excellent idea for this book and to Randy and Charlie for their collaboration. We stayed the course.

I am grateful to authors Terence Real, Susan Forward, Paul Kivel, Michael S. Kimmel, Lundy Bancroft, Ellen Pense, and Michael Paymar, whose work has furthered my education in the study of the male personality and the dynamics of domestic abuse. Thanks also to Karen Chernyaev, senior acquisitions editor at Hazelden Publishing and Educational Services, for her calm and even-tempered assistance.

I extend my heartfelt gratitude to my sister Irene, and to Marie, Marjorie, Maud, and Betty for their continued love and support, and my love and thanks to my daughter Claire, who has been with me as this book took shape and waited patiently as it took up my time. Finally, I want to thank my mother, whom I miss always, and without whose model of strength and perseverance I could never have made it this far.

Preface

We have over twenty-five years' combined experience working with men who abuse women. Often, our memories of the individuals—their personalities and offenses—fade with time, but the knowledge of the harm they've done stays with us.

Some of the men in our groups are angry, aggressive, and antisocial. They use women carelessly and callously, and they have little interest in establishing real relationships. Other men want their partners to be happy; they dream of creating stable and loving homes. They truly want to love the women in their lives. Yet they too hurt their partners—emotionally and physically—and in spite of their remorse, many of them are abusive and violent again and again. Our book is for this second group.

When we work with these men, who too often sabotage their relationships, when we prepare workshops on domestic abuse for other therapists, and when we wrote this book, we repeatedly ask ourselves two questions: Why do these men abuse their partners? How can we help them to stop? We hope our answers to these questions will give men the knowledge, inspiration, and drive to stop hurting the women they love.

During the last several years, we've noticed more and

more books for women who've been abused, as well as books for therapists who work with men who abuse. Since there is no book that approaches the men themselves in an inviting but challenging manner, we have written *Stop Hurting the Woman You Love*. While it is aimed at men who abuse, it also includes information helpful to victims and survivors as well as behavioral health professionals and court and law enforcement personnel.

Here are a few other things we want to point out.

The people depicted in the client stories are fictional compilations, and any similarity with real persons is coincidental.

This book deals solely with abusive heterosexual men. We are certainly aware that domestic abuse is a problem among gay and lesbian couples, but we see that as a topic for another book. In the same way, *Stop Hurting the Woman You Love* isn't designed to address men who are victims of domestic abuse. This is an important issue as well, but outside the scope of this particular book.

We are trained in and subscribe to the Domestic Abuse Intervention Program, better known as the Duluth Model, for working with men who abuse women. The fundamental tenet of the Duluth Model is: *Safety for the victim, accountability for the abusive man.* In this book, we have worked to portray the suffering of women and children at the hands of men who abuse, and we've attempted to avoid any statements or implications that would put women at risk. At the same time, we have endeavored to address men with respect, remembering that they are human beings who can change and be accountable for their behavior. They can stop hurting the women they love.

Finally, a remark to women whose partners read this book. We believe that reading *Stop Hurting the Woman You Love* will be helpful to many men. We hope that reading this book will encourage the man in your life to reduce or even eliminate his abusive behavior. However, it needs to be read in combination with treatment for domestic abuse, support group meetings, and the establishment of strong relationships with accountability partners. Even with these sources of accountability and support, men can relapse into emotional and physical violence. We therefore urge you to be vigilant and to take measures to increase your safety by getting information and support from your local women's shelter.

Randy Flood

Charlie Donaldson

Read Me First!

Y ou're stuck in traffic. You try to look around the truck in front of you, but you can't see what's holding things up. You feel the pump of adrenaline as you get more upset—you're going to be late for work. You are already angry and upset over last night's fight with the woman in your life. Traffic has stopped completely, but you can't stop the thoughts racing through your mind. Why do you argue so much? Why do you end up yelling at each other? Why can't you just get along? Your life seems gridlocked.

The truck ahead finally inches forward. You run through the recent history of your relationship: the angry voices, threats, ultimatums, stony silences. Sometimes it seems as if you and your partner have the same argument over and over. You're angry, but most of all you are tired.

You are not always sure what happens. The arguments seem to come out of nowhere. The night before you told your wife you were going to a bar with friends. You weren't planning on being out all night; you just wanted to relax and have a few drinks. She wanted you to stay home and help your ten-year-old son with his homework. You ended up screaming at her, telling her you never get to do any-thing and that living with her is like a life sentence in hell. You called her a few spiteful names, and she walked out of

1

the room with tears in her eyes. You don't want to talk to her that way, but the words just spill out. You've grabbed and pushed her before, and you were afraid last night that you might do it again. Or worse.

You're shocked at your own behavior, and you know you have to do something. Much as you hate to admit it, you know you need some help.

If your relationship is rocky because of domestic abuse—and especially if you have been violent with the woman in your life or you worry that you might be—this book is for you. If your partner has left you because of domestic abuse, then this book will help you to avoid the behavior that caused her to leave and will help you in your next relationship. Over the course of the thirteen chapters, we will

- help you to understand why you emotionally or physically hurt your partner
- give you down-to-earth tools to avoid domestic abuse
- assist you in developing a plan to create a more satisfying and healthy relationship

You will find a time-out plan that really works, questions that help you to explore what kind of man you are, and sensible techniques to improve your relationship and make you feel better about yourself and your life.

We have more than twenty-five years' combined experience running groups for men who have abused their partners and have sometimes been violent with them. We've worked with hundreds of men from all walks of life. Many of these men have been ordered by the court to attend our sessions as part of their probation agreement. On their first day in group, they're usually angry that they have to sit in a room with other men once a week for six months to talk about themselves and their relationships. Many men begin by blaming their partners and minimizing their abuse. But as the weeks pass, they begin to admit that physical abuse—whether a man has threatened his wife, pushed her, or hit her hard enough to break her jaw—is serious business. And many of them eventually understand that they are responsible for the violence in their homes.

The men in our groups also begin to recognize the destructiveness of their verbal and emotional abuse. Even when their behavior doesn't lead to physical injury or divorce, their constant criticism and humiliation deeply injure their partners. Once a man has emotionally or physically abused his partner, the relationship is never the same. Abuse creates a chasm between partners. It erodes trust that may take years to rebuild. In a minute—even a few seconds—everything changes.

You may be thinking, *Okay, but what about her?* In our work with abusive men, we often hear them say, "Well, she hit me first." We know that not all abuse is perpetrated by men against women. We recognize that wives and girlfriends can hurt men. But our goal is to help you take the first steps toward stopping your abusive behavior and creating a loving and healthy relationship. This book is designed especially to help men like you avoid abusing their intimate partners. You are not alone.

Three requests.

First, throughout this book you will find exercises and questions to help you examine your behavior. Invest in yourself: take the time to respond carefully. You will learn important things about yourself.

Second, this book is not intended to stand alone. We encourage you to participate in group or individual counseling with a therapist who has specialized training and experience in working with men who have abused their partners. If you are fearful that you may injure your partner, we urge you to get professional help immediately. You can also log on to our Web site, www.menscenter.org, for further information. The "Resources" section at the end of the book lists reading materials and additional Web sites.

Third, we ask that you read this book with courage and determination. If you are like many men, you are probably angry with your partner and blame her for provoking you to abuse. Throughout this book we will continually ask you to do something that is difficult and sometimes painful: to change your focus and take a look at yourself and your behavior. We know from our experience working with men like you that you are up to the task.

Although men who attend our treatment groups initially resist exploring their attitudes and behavior, many end up finding the process to be worthwhile and make significant changes in their lives. Many report that they are less abusive, argue on fewer occasions, communicate more deeply, and are happier in their relationships. Some make temporary changes and then fall back into abusive behaviors. Others approach their lives with a new sense of accountability and diligence. Most important, many of these men avoid violence.

We know that you may sometimes feel like flushing this book down the toilet. Don't. It will plug up your toilet, and your life and relationships will only get worse.

chapter one

It Started So Well

Bob, a quiet and soft-spoken man, seems out of place in Charlie's domestic abuse treatment group. While most men blame their partners for having to attend the group, Bob has said little about Daisy's role in landing him in court for domestic assault. But his story is typical in other ways.

"I wanted Daisy the moment I laid eyes on her," Bob remembers. "I don't mean I just wanted to sleep with her, although that's all I thought about for the first couple of weeks. What I mean is that I wanted her to be my wife. I wanted her in my life permanently. I was a happy man the day we married. Everything was fine for three or four years."

Bob is quiet for a moment. He shifts in his chair. The other men in the group wait patiently; most of them know what Bob will say next because they have said it themselves. "I don't know when things started to go wrong," Bob continues quietly. "It was just little things at first. She started getting on my nerves. When we were first married she'd usually go along with what I wanted. We never argued much. But after a while we started to disagree more and more, and I got tired of trying to explain my point of view to her. I mean, how many times can you repeat the same thing?"

Charlie asks Bob to explain one of these repetitive arguments.

"Well, for the first two years we were married we lived in an apartment, and we always spent Thanksgiving with her folks. That was okay with me because my family lives about six hours away. But after we bought our house, she insisted on having her family—all sixteen of them—to our house for Thanksgiving dinner. I didn't mind having them over, but I explained over and over that I really didn't want to be Mr. Host. She wanted me to talk to her sisters' husbands, make sure everyone had something to drink during the game, that sort of thing. I mean, it was a *holiday*—all I wanted to do was eat and watch football like everybody else. We had the same stupid argument for about three years. It always started out as a discussion, but it always ended up in an argument."

Bob slumps in his chair. "I don't see why she couldn't go along with me. It really wasn't that important."

"Having her family over was important to Daisy," Charlie points out. "So what happened last November?"

"There's not much to tell. We argued again, but it was different this time. She raised her voice, and I started shouting, too. I suddenly found myself holding her by both arms, shaking her. She screamed at me to let her go. I put my hand over her mouth to keep her from yelling, and all of a sudden, I realized what I was doing and let her go. She ran out to the garage, locked herself in the car, and called 911 on her cell phone."

"So here I am."

Bob's story is not unusual. Some of his experiences may be similar to yours. Like him, your relationship with your wife or girlfriend probably began on a positive and happy note. Being with her was easy; she made you feel good about yourself. For a while, life only seemed to get better. You thought about her all day long and couldn't wait to see her in the evening. Sex was great. Life was good.

Something Happened

But after a while—maybe months, maybe years—something seemed to go wrong. You didn't always want to do the same things or go to the same places, and your disagreements turned into arguments. Your disputes grew louder and more frequent. It seemed as if she deliberately did things to irritate you. She spent hours on the phone talking to friends. She seemed more interested in the kids than in you, and sometimes she didn't pay attention to you at all. She lost interest in sex—in fact, you hardly had any sex life at all.

Your life with her deteriorated to the point that some nights you didn't even want to go home. When you did arrive home, there were explosive arguments. And you found yourself yelling at her, perhaps calling her names and criticizing her. You may have threatened her. And one day, like Bob, you found yourself going over the edge: you grabbed her by the arms, or pushed her hard against the wall, or perhaps you even hit her. Whatever you did, it scared her. She didn't trust you anymore. And you knew you had gone too far.

You were probably shocked by your behavior. Your violence seemed sudden and uncontrollable. You felt guilty and you promised yourself, and her, that you would never behave like that again. And then . . . maybe . . . you did.

You knew you wanted to stop.

That Something Is You

But what happened to the good times? How did a relationship that began with love and mutual commitment disintegrate into arguing, name-calling, pushing, and hitting? Most men have their ups and downs, and coming home after work to a weed-choked lawn, too many bills, a whining toddler, and an indifferent wife might irritate any man. But you are more than irritated. The problem you are experiencing goes deeper than that. When things don't go the way you think they should, you sometimes find yourself in a sudden rage, and you want to blame her for making you angry.

You may think, "Why should I have to work so hard when she can't even keep the house clean? Why doesn't she understand that Sunday is my only day off and I shouldn't have to waste it at her mother's for dinner? Why does she always criticize my drinking when all I want is a couple of beers to calm myself down?" If she would do what you wanted her to, you may think, the arguments would stop. If she would stop making you so angry, you wouldn't find yourself on the verge of pushing or hitting her.

So you tell her that you want a clean house, that you don't want to go to her mother's, that you have a right to drink a few beers. But she doesn't get the message. When talking doesn't work, you try raising your voice to get her attention and make her agree with you. Maybe you shout and slam your fist on the table. Maybe you storm around the house but refuse to talk. You insult her, criticize her behavior, call her names, and eventually, perhaps, you grab, push, hit, or choke her. Domestic violence is the ultimate way of letting her know that she'd better pay attention to you.

Some men think that unless they have actually hit their partner, they are not guilty of abuse. No one calls 911 when they threaten or insult or yell at their wives or girlfriends. "If the police aren't standing in my living room," a man may think, "how could I be accused of abuse?" But abuse takes many forms. Domestic violence that results in a physical attack on your partner is one obvious form of abuse, but behavior that threatens, intimidates, or constantly demeans your partner is also abusive. In fact, for many women the scars of emotional abuse often last longer than those of physical abuse.

There Is Hope

You already know that to have a happy and healthy relationship, you will need to avoid emotional abuse and domestic violence. We don't need to tell you that. And you probably suspect that to revive the love and happiness you once felt and to regain your partner's trust and affection you will need to make some major changes in your life.

We want to help you with those changes, not only because you may be able to salvage your present relationship or avoid torpedoing a new one, but because it is the right thing to do. Hurting our partners, physically or emotionally, is never justifiable.

"Changing your behavior" doesn't mean turning yourself into a saint. The changes we're talking about involve taking control of your life so that you can be the man you want to be. It means being the best part of you. It means learning to respect the woman in your life by seeing her as a person like you. You can have a loving, trusting relationship unmarred by physical or emotional abuse.

You may think, "But what about her? Shouldn't she have to change? She could certainly stand some improvement!" It's true that she could probably change; most of us could improve our behavior. *But if you are serious about avoiding domestic violence and saving your relationship, the changes will need to start with you.* And the truth is you can't make her change. You can only change your own behavior. Although domestic abuse damages your partner and your relationship, healing begins when you take responsibility for your behavior and start on the journey of personal change.

If your partner has already left you because of domestic abuse, you are faced with the probability that no amount of change and good behavior on your part will bring her back. A relationship that has suffered serious abuse sometimes cannot be healed. But you probably don't want to live alone for the rest of your life. Sooner or later another woman will catch your eye, and when she returns your glance, you will want to be ready to begin a relationship without the shadow of domestic abuse. If your partner is still with you and remains committed to working on your relationship, then the success of your commitment depends on your willingness to work on you.

Your act of emotional or physical violence may seem to have come out of nowhere, happening so suddenly that you couldn't control it. But in fact, you can learn to understand and change the attitudes and beliefs that lead to abuse. You can let go of trying to control her and instead control yourself. This is the work that will keep you from hurting your partner again.

But learning how to control yourself takes time. If you are concerned that you may be violent with your partner *now*, the next chapter offers short-term suggestions for avoiding domestic violence.

chapter two

The Time-Out
Avoiding Violence *Now*

If you have been violent in your relationship or if you are concerned you may be violent, you have one goal that ranks above all the rest: to avoid physically hurting your partner. In the long run, you'll probably need to make some changes to avoid emotional abuse—yelling at her or insulting, criticizing, or threatening her. But if violence threatens your relationship *right now,* then avoiding physical abuse is your top priority. It is the most important thing you can do.

The purpose of the time-out is to prevent domestic violence. Some men can remain in the same room with their partners during an argument without becoming abusive. Others have more trouble managing their feelings and behavior, and they need to physically leave to avoid violence and abuse.

If you have been violent with your partner or are concerned that you may be, then both of you will benefit from the time-out technique. The time-out is intended to let you remove yourself from a potentially explosive confrontation before you become violent. It is not designed as a long-term solution. Instead, the time-out is a stopgap measure devised to give you the time you need to control your behavior.

Violence: The Last Step in a Process

Domestic violence doesn't just happen. It is supported by an unseen foundation of boyhood experiences and a man's sense of *entitlement,* his belief that a woman should go along with what he wants. The final steps leading up to violence often involve a series of interactions between the two of you. That process can start when you try to persuade your partner to do something.

Let's say, for example, that you want her to agree that you should get a new truck. She refuses, insisting that you need a new van for the family instead of a pickup. When asking doesn't get what you want, you start to insist, perhaps loudly or with threats, that she agree. But she *still* won't go along with you. Her refusal can stir up old feelings of hurt and rejection. "Why don't I ever get what I want around here? Why is it always the family first, regardless of what I need?" you may think to yourself. "Why doesn't she ever understand that I need things, too?" At this point, the steps in the domestic violence process zip by with dizzying speed.

Your hurt feelings are so uncomfortable that they barely register before you convert them to anger. Anger is an easier emotion to handle because it doesn't make you feel bad, at least not at first. Anger lets you feel more in control. Anger gives you power; it lets you feel justified. So when you angrily tell her, for the last time, that you're going to get a truck no matter what she says, you reinforce your message with physical violence.

How can you stop yourself from getting caught in this tornado? What can you do to save your relationship rather than destroy it with violence? You can learn that you are not entitled to always get your way. You can become less demanding and controlling. You can learn to negotiate. And you can learn to be less angry.

But all those changes take time . . . months, and probably years. And you don't have that much time. In the middle of an escalating confrontation, you have only a few precious minutes in which to alter the final stages in the domestic violence process. If you've been working on getting along better with your partner, the gains you have made in improving your relationship will be lost if you hit or choke or punch or kick or push her even once more. To avoid more physical abuse, you need something that you can do *now*—a self-stopping technique that will allow you to control yourself and keep you from committing a violent act. The best thing you can do is to *get the hell out of there* when you think you might become violent. It's like hitting the eject button before your plane crashes. If your plane is losing altitude, you need to get out before you hit the ground. The two of you will probably parachute to different places, but at least you won't crash with the airplane.

Your Best Defense

Taking a time-out is like hitting that eject button. It is your best defense against yourself—the hurt, angry, violent you. Used properly, the time-out can prevent you from committing an act of domestic violence and can contribute to a healthy relationship. It is a way of honoring yourself and maintaining the safety of your partner.

The time-out is not a new idea. You may even have tried it before. But you may not have used it effectively, and your partner may not have liked you walking out on her. In the middle of a hot argument, you may have shouted, "This is ridiculous—I'm out of here!" and slammed out of the house. But whatever you were talking about wasn't resolved. Your partner felt cut off and discounted, and you probably came back pretending that nothing had happened, making things even worse.

You may say, "Well, what if she hits me first? She needs to take the time-out!" We know that some women can be aggressive and violent, but you are probably much stronger than your partner is, and therefore more capable of injuring her. Even if both of you are physically aggressive, you're the one who is more likely to cause significant injury. So the time-out becomes your responsibility.

Finding Your Exit Point

To use the time-out properly, some preparation is needed. First, you need to identify your exit point. Second, you need to request your partner's cooperation.

The exit point is the moment at which you can still get yourself to leave to avoid hurting the woman you love. Once your anger has boiled beyond your control, it will be much harder to stop yourself from completing the steps in the domestic violence process. Anger doesn't *cause* violence, but it can exaggerate your feelings of hurt or entitlement when your partner doesn't behave the way you want her to.

To identify your personal exit point, you need an internal anger thermometer.

The scale on the thermometer below goes from 0 (freezing) to 100 (boiling). Most men call the range from *20 to 40 degrees* irritation: your brother-in-law who knows everything won't stop talking; you need four-by-fours cut at the lumberyard and no one seems to be working there.

At *60 degrees* you are probably angry: you feel justified in telling off a co-worker who has taken credit for your work, even though you know it will cause trouble at your job; you bark at your wife when she tells you that you need to take care of the kids when you'd planned to play golf.

By the time your thermometer hits *80 degrees,* your rage is hot enough for you to break things and hurt people: you have upended the kitchen table and are ready to punch your wife if she crosses you.

At *100 degrees* an angry, violent man can kill someone.

You can begin to understand your pattern of anger by using the thermometer to help you identify which situations merely annoy you, which ones make you angry, and which ones make you want to hit someone. Understanding how and when you get angry is important because anger increases the likelihood of violence. If you don't know which situations set you off, you won't be able to control your responses to them.

Consider your level of irritation, anger, or rage in the following situations and pick a number between 0 and 100 for each.

- The car in front of you on the freeway is driving 20 miles per hour **under** the speed limit.
- Your boss **criticizes** you unfairly.
- You come home after taking your girlfriend out for a romantic dinner and she **refuses** to make love.
- Your son calls you a **prick.**
- The house is a **mess** when you get home from work.
- You think your partner has **cheated** on you.
- A careless driver bumps into your car and **dents** your trunk.

These are only a few examples. You can modify and add to them until you have a list of incidents that accurately represents what angers you. Write the most irritating of these situations beside the thermometer.

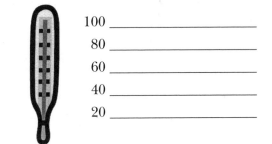

100 _____

80 _____

60 _____

40 _____

20 _____

Now think about a time you abused your partner—a time when you lost control and did something that scared or hurt her. Maybe you yelled or threw something, or perhaps you actually hit, grabbed, or shoved her. Recall how you felt at that time. Remember how angry you were. What were you thinking? How did your body feel? No doubt your muscles were tight; your whole body felt tense. Your heart was beating fast.

Now think a little further back, and **recall the moment when you could have chosen to leave before you became abusive.** How angry were you then? What was your anger temperature at that moment? **This is your exit point.** Put your exit point temperature on the thermometer and circle it.

Most men say that their exit point falls somewhere between 50 and 70 degrees. They find that below 50 they can manage their feelings and that above 70 it's probably too late.

Using the Time-Out

The time-out process involves six steps, each of which needs to be followed or the time-out will not work. We've used the word **TEMPER** to make the steps easier to remember.

T—Take your temperature. Find out if you are at or near your exit point temperature. If you are, proceed with the time-out.

E—Explain to your partner that you need to take a time-out. Let her know you are concerned that if you stay any longer, you may not be able to manage your behavior.

M—Mention exactly how many minutes you'll be gone. We suggest thirty to sixty minutes.

P—Promise to return. Tell her that you know your discussion is important and that you want to try to resolve the issue.

E—Exit. Leave your home. Going to the basement or

garage is not adequate. Use calm breathing and positive self-talk to help quiet yourself and let go of your anger. It may help to take a walk or do another form of exercise. Do not go to a bar, casino, or any other place that interferes with your calming down and thinking clearly.

R—Return at the designated time and continue the discussion. If the time-out hasn't been long enough to let you calm down, then explain to your partner that you need more time. Take another time-out. Once again, let her know how long you will be gone, and promise to return. Returning on time is important; if you don't, your partner is unlikely to believe you the next time.

A successful time-out won't happen by itself. It requires thinking through the steps and how you plan to implement them.

Josh, one of Randy's clients, complained bitterly in group about the ineffectiveness of the time-out after being arrested for domestic violence. Randy started counseling Josh individually to help Josh gain an understanding of his problems.

Josh and his partner, Melissa, frequently argued about their son, Daniel, who was skipping school and failing several courses. Josh wanted to discipline Daniel his way by taking Daniel's car away permanently; Melissa thought the car should be used as a reward for getting passing grades. During one of their intense confrontations, Josh found himself yelling at the top of his lungs and pounding his fist on the table. He knew that his temperature was rising and realized that he was past his exit point. He shouted at Melissa, "I'm getting out of here!" as he turned to leave.

Melissa stepped quickly between Josh and the door. "You never finish these discussions. God, you are gutless! You always leave before we get anywhere."

Josh screamed, "Screw you!" and pushed her back several steps into the wall. She grabbed his wrist and he backhanded her, giving her a black eye before storming out to his car. Melissa called 911; Josh was arrested for domestic violence when he returned home.

"Josh was humiliated by his arrest," Randy recalls. "He was furious with me, with Melissa, and with the whole idea of counseling. I thought he would quit, but he continued his sessions, and eventually we were able to work on the time-out so that he could implement all the steps. But you know what? He never needed to use it again. Just being able to identify his exit point was enough to let him stay in the room when he and Melissa argued."

When Josh did not keep track of his temperature and leave before he reached his exit point, it was almost inevitable that he would omit two important steps: **M** (mention how long you'll be gone) and **P** (promise to return). Unfortunately, these are the two most frequently overlooked steps.

It is absolutely essential to say how long you will be gone and promise to return. Failing to do so sets the stage for domestic violence, as it did for Josh. If you don't say how long you will be gone and promise to return, your partner almost certainly will feel that you are escaping to avoid the discussion. She will feel discounted and disrespected, and in her hurt and anger, she may try to block you from leaving, as Melissa did. Because you believe she doesn't have the right to make you stay, your anger could escalate still further. You might hit or grab her, scaring her and creating another wall in your relationship. And like Josh, you may also find yourself in jail.

Abusing the Time-Out

You need to use the time-out carefully and accountably. Some men abuse the time-out by using it as a convenient means to get what they want. Mike, who attended one of Charlie's groups, liked to pick a fight with his wife, Beth, and then use the time-out as a way to get out of the house and have a few drinks with his buddies on Thursday nights. Almost any subject could provide an excuse for an argument: Beth spent too much time at work and was neglecting the house, the kids, and him; she didn't get estimates for a new roof, which he had told her to do; she talked to her nosy, interfering sister too much. Mike knew exactly which subjects would get an angry response from Beth. He could easily start an argument, call for a time-out, and then leave the house.

Used in an accountable manner, the time-out gives you the time you need to control yourself and avoid violence. Used irresponsibly, the time-out is a cheap trick that lets you evade responsibility and duck unpleasant but necessary discussions with your partner.

Ask for Your Partner's Help

If you want to use the time-out as a tool to avoid violence, you need to tell your partner about it first. Don't spring it on her when things have already heated up and you feel you need to leave. Ask her if she wants to talk about the use of a time-out. If she does, ask her to read this chapter. Pick a time when you are both calm and relaxed, and explain that you want to start using the time-out technique described in this book. Remember that without her agreement, using a time-out is an act of control. Let her know

- that you know you've been abusive in the past, that you're sorry, and that you are working to avoid hurting her physically or emotionally in the future
- that you want to use the time-out because you don't want to be abusive and violent

- that you will use the time-out only when you really need to, and that you won't use it as a tactic of control or a way of getting out of an argument or a difficult discussion
- that you know walking out in the middle of an argument is disrespectful, and that in the future, when you need to leave to calm down, you will promise to return and continue the discussion at the agreed-upon time

If your partner says she doesn't believe you or trust you, don't argue with her. She probably has good reason to question your integrity. Rather than insisting that you have changed, simply tell her that you will work on being more trustworthy.

What If She Doesn't Want Me to Take a Time-Out?

If you need to use a time-out, but your partner persists in the argument and tells you that she doesn't want you to leave, it's probably because you haven't listened to her or been emotionally available for a long time. She may be frustrated because you haven't been attentive to her or what she has to say. She feels discounted, and she may have reached the point where she demands you listen to her legitimate requests for you to stay in spite of your decision that you need to take a time-out.

In this case, your best choice is to stay put and find an internal rather than an external space to calm down. Breathe deeply and slowly; remind yourself that you have had arguments before during which you were not physically violent and that you can do it again.

Lower your voice: if you don't shout, she may calm down, too. You can also listen to what she says and try to respond to her. You may find that the tension lessens and you feel able to stay without the threat of violence. Other suggestions for managing your thoughts and feelings are discussed in chapter 7.

But if you are close to your exit point temperature and she insists that you stay, you need to decide if you are truly in jeopardy of hurting her or if you can control yourself in the situation. If you honestly believe you will physically harm her if you don't take a time-out, we recommend that you leave.

What If She Blocks Me from Leaving?

The men who attend our groups have committed a wide range of violent acts, including pushing a partner who has tried to block them when they wanted to leave.

Ray, a welder who worked on the superstructure of highrise office buildings, was a big guy who got his way and was known as a bully with his crew. He had been in Randy's group for only a few weeks when he and his wife Patricia got into a heated argument about the amount of money she spent on clothes. Ray had learned the basics of the time-out technique, but it was hard for him to admit that he needed to know his exit point temperature because he was used to getting hotter and hotter until he got what he wanted. But during the argument Ray did manage to realize he was letting himself get too worked up. He tried to calm himself enough to tell Patricia that he needed a time-out, and unlike Josh, he remembered to tell his wife that he would leave for one hour and then return to continue the discussion if they were both calmed down. But Patricia was too angry to listen. "I'm sick of this crap," she stormed. "We're going to finish this discussion now." Ray started to leave, but Patricia jumped between him and the door. That was too much for Ray.

"Nobody's going to keep me from leaving," he yelled. He grabbed her by the shoulders, slammed her into the wall, and left.

There are several ways to avoid an outcome like Ray's. If you feel you must leave to protect your partner's safety, try to exit by another door. Or put your hands to your sides and move out of her presence. If she grabs or hits you, simply keep moving. It's unlikely that she will physically be able to stop you from leaving. Men who are violent while attempting to take a time-out have a choice, but they let their machismo and sense of entitlement determine their behavior.

The Last Resort

The time-out is a stopgap measure. If your airplane is spinning out of control, it's only a matter of time before it crashes nose-first into the ground, so it makes sense to hit the eject button before that happens. But you don't want to rely on a parachute for the rest of your life. With time, a strong desire to change, and the support of those around you, you will learn to pilot the plane so that you never need the last resort of the eject button.

The time-out is a tool you should always have with you, but it's one you hope you'll never have to use.

Anger as a tactic of control

Men often think of anger as something that simply happens to them. When they abuse their partners, it seems like somebody else takes over, and their violence comes out of nowhere. In fact, human beings have considerable control of their anger and the thinking that creates it. But some men intentionally choose not to control their anger because they know they're likely to get what they want if they stay angry. Unchecked anger is a tactic of control. When a man scares his partner with his rage, she's more likely to do what he wants. Punishing her with threats and intimidation for not doing what he wants makes her more likely to comply in the future.

If men want to be respectful partners and develop healthy relationships, they need to let go of both the sense of entitlement that they have the right to get their way and the deliberate anger that they use to get what they want.

Some men don't get angry. They don't feel the blood coursing through their veins or the hair bristling on the backs of their necks. They remain serene, and they actually become detached and distant when things don't go their way. Although they behave as if they're angry and can be violent in their abuse, inside they are calm and deliberate and very much in control. If you're one of these men, you are probably emotionally shut down. You need to work on getting in touch with your feelings, particularly your feeling of empathy for your partner. You probably need some help with this. Make an appointment with a therapist who specializes in men's work and domestic violence. You owe it to your partner and yourself.

chapter three

Five Lies That Ruin Lives

The bottom line is this: your life hasn't been going well because your relationship with your wife or girlfriend is rocky. Perhaps you're not in a relationship at all because you've been abusive in the past. Even the successes in your life seem threatened by your relationship problems. Your co-workers like you and your boss praises your job performance, but sometimes you feel that life at work will spin out of control if you have one more argument at home. You and your wife or girlfriend disagree about almost anything. You're often angry and frustrated. She talks about breaking up; you've threatened her and maybe pushed or shaken her. Perhaps the two of you have already split up, or you've been arrested for domestic violence.

But you're a bright and practical guy. You understand how computers and cars work, or at least enough to make them work for you. You're perceptive; you know when to ask for a raise, and you can solve problems with co-workers. But this problem, the biggest problem in your life—your relationship—you haven't solved. And there's a good chance that in spite of all you know, in spite of the fact that you're a sound thinker and make good decisions, you don't think very clearly about your relationship with the woman in your life. Your thinking may be so distorted that you've made some

24

poor choices. You may have decided to yell at her because you think she deserves it, or you may believe that you can have an affair and no one will get hurt. Later you may have realized that your actions didn't get the results you wanted, but you've fallen into the same trap of distorted thinking time and again.

We're going to tell you an important truth here, a truth that you need to fully understand if you want to improve your life:

When you engage in distorting thinking you are lying to yourself.

Worse, often you don't recognize the lie. Distorted thinking allows you to believe one of the most basic lies that we tell ourselves—*that the world should be a certain way*—and you make misguided choices as a result of trying to make the world fit the lie. Consider a simple example. The driver who believes he has a right to drive on the freeway without being cut off by other drivers believes a lie. He may not be aware of this lie/belief, but you can tell by his behavior that he lives by it. If you try to move into the outside lane before you reach your exit, he will speed up to block you. If you need to merge because construction has reduced two lanes to one, he will not let you in. His thinking is distorted by his belief in the lie that the world should be a certain way. In this case, he believes the lie that you don't have a right to get into his lane if he is inconvenienced for a nanosecond. His behavior behind the wheel is the result of his distorted thinking.

When you believe that the world should be a certain way, then it's only a short step to believing that the woman in your life should behave in certain ways. When she doesn't behave the way you want her to, distorted thinking inevitably leads to the conclusion that she is to blame for the trouble in your relationship and your life.

For abusive men, the lie that the world should conform

to their wishes usually takes five forms. You may not have told yourself all five lies, but any one of them can lead you to destructive or abusive behavior that can only harm yourself and the woman you love. The lies are about issues of change and control in your relationship. As you read this chapter, think about how often you find one of these lies spiraling through your mind, pulling you toward abuse and violence. We believe that you can deconstruct the lies—pull them apart—and become aware of them so that you do not tell them to yourself. When you can see the lie, then seeing the truth will be much easier, and you can learn to avoid the damage that living the lie creates.

Lie #1: I Can Still Live Like a Single Man

Most of you had pretty good lives before you met your partners. You hunted and fished with your buddies, spent every spare minute on the golf course, got the latest computer equipment, and flirted with every other woman you saw. It was fun. It was simple. There were a lot of rewards and perks to the single life, and you took advantage of them.

Then you met the woman who, perhaps too soon, became the mother of your children. She wanted shared household responsibilities, family time, and a van. You wanted to keep living the single life you enjoyed before you married, spending your time and money on golf, hunting, and the latest computer gadgets.

Eventually, the disagreements between you and your wife caused tremors, maybe even a small earthquake. She wanted you to go to her mother's for dinner every Sunday; you wanted to play golf. She said, "The kids need new school clothes"; you said, "I need a new scanner."

The truth? You are no longer single. You cannot be in a committed relationship and continue to live like a single man. Your wife and family need and deserve some of your time. Bringing home a paycheck is not enough to meet their needs. Giving your family your time and attention doesn't mean you never get to play golf, but it does mean you may not be able to tee off every Sunday afternoon.

Mitch had agreed to a family picnic for Memorial Day. His two sons knew that their dad sometimes made promises to his family that he didn't keep, but they were excited because Mitch had said they could each bring a friend, which was unusual. The boys were certain that their dad wouldn't cancel with two guests invited. That morning, thinking of the noise and confusion and inevitable spats among the four boys, Mitch decided he'd rather spend the day working on his vintage Corvette. After breakfast, he started an argument with Rose, his wife, accusing her of talking too much on the phone. When Rose defended herself, he accused her of being "emotional" and said he didn't want to spend the day with someone who got upset so easily. Mitch got what we wanted; he put a new exhaust system on his car. He also further damaged his relationship with his wife and sons, who knew he had broken his promise to go to the picnic.

Ask yourself:

- Am I living the lie that I am still a single man?
- Or do I willingly give my time and attention to make my relationship work?

Lie #2: If She Would Change, Then Everything Would Be Better

When something goes wrong, too often we want to blame someone else.

Picture Randy and Charlie giving one of their workshops on men's issues. In an elegant hotel conference room with glittering chandeliers and thick, sculpted carpet, in front of a hundred other therapists, Charlie discovers the PowerPoint slides are out of order. He automatically blames Randy. "If he didn't always wait until the last minute, then we'd have time to check these things," Charlie grumbles to himself, feeling anger well up inside him. The truth? Charlie had volunteered to check the slides, but in the midst of his embarrassment at the mistake, he overlooks this truth.

Similarly, when things aren't going well in your relationship, you may blame your partner and want her to change. Maybe you want her to stop nagging, to let you off the hook when you promised to get home for dinner at seven and you show up after nine, or to forget that *you* forgot your wedding anniversary. Everything would be better if only she'd change.

Charlie's client, Paul. Paul was angry. He had been in counseling for a year, and on this day he walked right past me, dispensing with his usual chat about the Pistons, and launched into an attack on his wife, Heather, before he'd even sat down.

"She doesn't want to have sex anymore, she won't go to Florida for our annual convention, she doesn't even greet me at the door." He paused, flushed, and I seized on the last of his accusations.

"So she doesn't even say hello?"

"No, she just keeps on reading the paper or cooking or whatever the hell she's doing."

"And that's not how you'd like her to behave."

Paul was still steamed. "Well, no, dammit. And I let her know it. I told her that if she couldn't at least get up and say hello to the man who's providing her with a house with a pool and a new Grand Am, she could find somebody else to do it."

"And how'd she react?" I asked.

Paul rolled his eyes and shrugged helplessly. "She starting crying and went into the bathroom."

"So you come home from work, you're tired, and you'd like some attention."

"Well," he slows down a bit. "I don't think it's attention, I'd just like . . ."

I interrupt him. "I think you'd like some attention. You want her to tell you she's glad to see you. You want her to make a fuss over you."

"You make me sound like a kid . . ." His voice trails off, and I can tell he knows what I'm talking about.

Paul's mother was an alcoholic. She started drinking at ten in the morning, and by the time he got home from school, she was often passed out on the couch, an empty fifth of gin on the coffee table. Paul would turn off the TV, go into the kitchen, pour himself a glass of milk, and eat a handful of cookies. Often that was dinner.

Paul and I had talked about his feelings of abandonment, and about how he brought those feelings into his relationship. He knew that he projected the hurt his mother caused him onto Heather, but he wasn't always aware when he did so. We talked for a while about how seeing Heather's actions through the filter of his mother's behavior distorted his perception of what was really going on.

When Paul had calmed down, he said, "You know, Heather does always give me a hug. And I know I'm lucky because she always does want to make love. It's just that . . . sometimes . . . it's not soon enough. I get upset so fast, and the bad thing is that I accuse her of being cold and uncaring. And she isn't." He stared at the floor.

"But you still want her to change," I tell him. "You want her to jump up the second you walk in the door and hold you and kiss you. But if you calm yourself down, you can remember that what you're really upset about is something that happened years ago, when your mother wasn't there, day after day, to greet you."

Paul looked up at me. "It's really about me, isn't it?"

"Yes," I said.

The truth that Paul was learning is that a man's desire to

change his partner's behavior reflects his needs far more than her behavior.

Paul would like Heather to change, and she could. She could greet him every day after work with a hug and plans for a romantic evening, but Paul, given his abandonment issues, would probably never feel really truly loved. Heather could dote on him constantly, but inevitably she'd neglect to do something—she'd forget to ask about his day or give him a kiss on the way out the door—and all the pain he felt as a boy would flood over him again. Paul needed to stay in counseling until *he changed himself*—until he learned to calm and soothe himself and convince himself that Heather's occasional small omissions weren't a sign that she didn't love him.

Some of us don't have the deep-seated issues that troubled Paul. But we do have plenty of problems—impatience, boredom, anger, depression, anxiety—and it's easy to want our partners to change to make our problems go away. If she were just different, we think, we'd stop getting so angry and we wouldn't argue so much. The truth? You cannot change other people.

No one likes being forced to change her behavior. Your partner will resist. She will fight back because she finds your attempts invasive and controlling. If *you* persist in believing the lie that she should change, you will grow increasingly angry and frustrated when *she* persists in her usual behavior. Your anger and frustration and the mistaken belief that she alone is responsible for the problems in your life can too easily lead to domestic abuse.

Ask yourself:

- Do I live by the lie that if my partner would change, then I wouldn't be angry and abusive, and therefore my life would be smoother?

- Or am I willing to change my own behavior and ways of looking at the world?

Lie #3: I Have a Right to Control Her

If you believe the lie that changing her will improve your life, and she resists your suggestions or threats that she should change, then your distorted thinking can lead to the next "logical" lie: I have a right to control her and make her do what I want. Just as your partner will almost always oppose your efforts to make her change, she will resist your attempts to control her. The outcome of controlling behavior can be devastating for both partners, as Stephen's story below shows.

Randy's client, Stephen. Stephen was a cop in the vice squad. Underneath the tough-guy image that he showed to drug runners as well as to other cops, he was a deeply insecure man. He'd met Linda, his pretty and outgoing wife, at a busy lunch counter. Linda smiled and made small talk as they waited in line, and by the time they finished lunch he had asked her out. Although it was clear to both of their families that Linda loved Stephen and never thought of straying, he worried about her having an affair and was jealous when he saw her talking with other men. He wanted to know where she was and when she would be home.

Linda worked as a medical transcriptionist in the suburb where they lived, and she liked to stop by a coffee shop on her way home. She got off work around five, and two or three nights a week she'd have a latte with her co-workers. When Stephen arrived home first, he'd worry about why she wasn't there. She was almost always home by 6:30, but for Stephen the time alone in their empty apartment seemed like a long, long time. He imagined her smiling at guys that came on to her, always remembering how he had met her and how she had responded to him. Stephen never understood that Linda's friendly, extroverted personality didn't mean that she would cheat on him.

Stephen repeatedly asked her to come home straight from work. One night when Linda didn't come home until seven, he sat at the kitchen table drinking beer. He grew more and more angry as he sat there, convinced she was having an affair. When he heard her key in the lock, he met her at the door, grabbed her by the arms, and roughly pulled her inside. He demanded the keys to her car and said that she wasn't allowed to go out anymore after work. When Linda tried to get away from him, Stephen pushed her hard against the wall. Her elbow was bruised so badly that she couldn't straighten her arm for a week.

Stephen was remorseful. He'd never meant to hurt her, but at the same time he believed that he did what he needed to do: he let her know that it would be best for her if she was home when he wanted her to be. Over the next few weeks Stephen and Linda made up, and he breathed a sigh of relief.

One day, a month later, Stephen came home to find Linda and all her things gone. Nothing of her remained. Her e-mail and files had been erased from the computer; the memory in the phone had been wiped clean. Stephen tried to call Linda's sister and her best friend, but the numbers had been changed, and information said their new numbers were unlisted. The next day Stephen was served with a personal protection order that forbade him to call Linda at work or to be within a hundred yards of her.

On the surface it may seem that if you control something you've got it, it's your possession, it's yours to keep. The truth? Ultimately, you will lose what you try to control. Maybe you meet a woman and right away she recognizes your attempt to make all the decisions and she never calls you back. Maybe you've told your wife what to do and not do for the past twenty years. One day you have an argument, and she tells you she's getting a divorce. The principle is simple: what you control, you lose. Even if your wife or girlfriend doesn't walk out, as Linda did, your push to control her will cause her to suffer a loss of spontaneity, joy, and love for you. When her life is diminished by your controlling behavior, you lose, too.

Ask yourself:

- Do I practice the lie that I have a right to control my partner?
- Or do I accept her as a person, not a possession, and understand that I do not have the right to threaten her or force her to change for my satisfaction?

Lie #4: If I Treat Her as an Equal, Then I'll No Longer Be in Control of My Life

It worked for a while. You called the shots and your girlfriend or wife went along. Like your father, you were the head of the household, and you made all the decisions. Maybe you didn't like her spending so much time on church projects. You told her to stop, and she did. You told her that you didn't like her hair, and she went blond. The kids were noisy and messy and you hate noise and disorder, so you told her to punish the kids, and she reluctantly agreed. For a while, you were in control: when you didn't like something, she changed. For six months or six years, you got what you wanted, and you stayed in control.

Then something happened. She met a woman who encouraged her to stand up for herself, or she just got fed up with deferring to you. She decided that she had some rights, too, and the arguing started. She said she wanted you to be home more in the evenings, to spend more time with the kids, to clean the house yourself if you didn't like how she did it. She said this was the twenty-first century and she didn't intend to be your maid any more.

You were angry. You were probably shocked, too, because things seemed to be going smoothly and you were unprepared for what seemed like a sudden rebellion. You made a lot more money than she did, and you thought it made sense for her to do a little more around the house. She said it wasn't "a little more" and that you needed to grow up or get some counseling.

You felt that if you gave in to her demands you wouldn't be a man. Your mother had done everything around the house—your dad sat in his lounge chair and watched the Yankees while she cooked, cleaned, washed dishes, did the laundry, took care of you and your siblings, and attended to all the details of running the household. You believe that this arrangement worked for your parents and that it should work for you. Your wife's refusal to go along with you made you feel disrespected, but in an effort to keep the peace you gave in and did the laundry occasionally, spent more time with the kids, and even took her out to dinner. But you resented your new duties, and she resented the fact that you didn't do enough. One day she said, "This isn't working." You replied, "You're right," already planning to find a woman who would give you the respect you thought you deserved.

Turning your marriage into a win/lose battlefield is the inevitable effect of the lie that says equality in a relationship will cause you to lose control. If you believe the lie, then your encounters with the woman in your life will frequently be tense. The lie sets up a false win/lose scenario: either she wins or I do; either she's in control or I am. But an intimate relationship doesn't have winners and losers. The desire to be in control at all times erodes the quality of our lives with our partners.

Ask yourself:
- Do I believe the lie that treating my partner as an equal in our relationship will result in a loss of control and respect?
- Or do I understand that by treating my partner as my equal and avoiding controlling and overbearing behavior, I will increase my chances of earning her love and respect?

Lie #5: I Just Can't Help Myself

When men enter our domestic abuse groups they often say that they didn't mean to hurt her; they just drank too much, or they were angry, or she'd been nagging them all day long, or she started it by hitting them first. Essentially, they argue that they are not to blame for hurting her because they didn't mean to and they couldn't stop themselves. Many of the men are angry and resentful at being forced to participate in a domestic abuse treatment program when they believe that they did not consciously intend to injure their partners.

Charlie's client, Jerry. Jerry didn't just resent attending the program—he was enraged. A construction worker who was used to yelling, Jerry told us in a very loud voice that they were arguing because Monica had wanted to take his truck to work, and she had hit him first, and *she* was the one who should have been arrested. In fact, he said, she had punched him three times on the face. He had hit her back once, and he now he was the one who had to come to this damn group. He'd always thought that Ottawa County had the worst courts in Michigan, and now he was sure of it.

Some of the other newer group members nodded in agreement. I looked around the room. Vince was now in his twenty-third week of the twenty-six-week program. I could tell he had something to say. He looked over at Jerry and asked him, "Jerry, how much do you weigh?"

It was clear to every man in the room that Jerry weighed well over 200 pounds. He answered, "About 250."

"And how much does Monica weigh?" Vince asked.

"Oh, she's pretty skinny," Jerry answered.

"What do you figure she weighs?" I asked.

"Maybe 110."

I couldn't help but ask, "Does she work out?"

"Nah," Jerry answered. "She's into that yoga stuff."

"So," I went on, "I'll bet you've got ten times the muscle mass that she has."

"Yeah, I guess so."

The heads that had been nodding in support of Jerry were now still. Bruce was new to the group but was catching on fast. "Did you get hurt? I mean, did she injure you?" he asked.

"No," Jerry said.

Bruce persisted. "How about her?"

"She had a broken nose."

Jerry couldn't see it, but everyone else in the room could. He hit Monica to let her know that she'd better not hit him. She had crossed a boundary—she had become too aggressive for his taste ("Nobody lays hands on me")—in spite of the fact that he could hardly feel her punches. He broke her nose to let her know who was in charge and that he was going to make the decisions. Three months passed before he acknowledged that *maybe* he had a choice about using aggressive physical force against his wife.

When we talk in group about Jerry's story, we first remind the guys that they are responsible for their behavior no matter what their partner does. Even if a man is in actual physical danger, he still has defensive choices other than pushing, punching, grabbing, or choking her. Ed's story clearly illustrates the "I had no choice" lie.

Randy's client, Ed. During Ed's intake assessment, he explained that he was arrested for domestic violence because he has a bad temper. "I just blow my cork sometimes," Ed said. He seemed to think his temper accounted for all his troubles.

"How often do you blow your cork at work?" I asked.

Ed responded indignantly. "I don't blow up at work!" He paused, and then added, "I used to yell at my co-workers, and even my boss once in a while, but I stopped."

"Why don't you yell at work anymore?"

"It almost got me fired," Ed muttered.

Despite his claim that he was arrested because he couldn't manage his temper, Ed could indeed control when he would "blow his cork." If he truly were unable to control himself, eventually he would have been fired. But the serious warnings he received at work were enough to make him cool down. Ed was able to manage his behavior at work because he knew he would be held accountable. Unfortunately for his wife, Ed did not feel compelled to control his temper at home. What we do with our loved ones when no one is looking says a lot about our character.

Ask yourself:

- Have I ever justified physically abusing my partner with the lie that I just couldn't help myself and that I just made a mistake when I hurt her?
- Or do I accept that domestic abuse is a choice that I can control and that it's never just a mistake?

One Unavoidable Truth

There's only one person you can change, and that person is you.

If you want to improve your life and relationship and enjoy more love and less strife, you need to concentrate on changing yourself, not her.

All the lies are about two fundamental aspects of human relationships: change and control. Like any lie involving human behavior, they are backward, twisted, and upside down. No wonder we have trouble with our relationships! Many men have lived with the burden of these lies for years.

But you can change these beliefs. You can ask yourself the hard questions listed above, and by thinking about your behavior you can slowly become aware of how the lies have distorted your thinking and your life. On the surface, the fact that you're the one who has to do the difficult work of changing can seem like bad news. You may fear the losses that sometimes come with change. You may not like to admit, even to yourself, that recognizing the need for change means admitting that you aren't perfect. But think about it for a minute. Really think about it, because this is a fundamental point: *If she's the one who has to change for your life to improve, then who's in charge? She is.* If she decides to change to meet your expectations, great. If she doesn't, you'll be trapped in the same arguments and anger and frustrations. If she has to change for your life to improve, then you're pretty much at her mercy.

If, on the other hand, you're the one who chooses to change, then you can improve your life no matter what she does. This is good news! It's empowering. Once Paul recognized that he didn't need to be caught by childhood pain and disappointment, he felt better because he knew he could think and feel and act differently. He was no longer so dependent on Heather, because he didn't need her to be perfect.

This book is about change. It won't be of much value if you read it from cover to cover and nothing different happens in your life. If you read this book looking for ways to change your partner so you don't get angry and abusive anymore, then you will miss the point. We hope you are reading with the idea that you can change some of your beliefs and behaviors. The biggest change you need to make is to forsake emotional and physical abuse. But you also need to change who you are in the relationship. You probably want the best for yourself and your wife and family. Now is the time to start acting like it. So what do you do next?

1. *Understand and accept that domestic abuse is a choice.* It's a time when you can be in control—not of her or the relationship—but of how you behave. Domestic abuse is a choice: reject it.

2. *Take responsibility for your actions and beliefs.* Reject the urge to blame others. Your partner isn't responsible for what you do. As a man who is capable of doing great harm to others, you need to be aware of and manage what you think, feel, say, and do. Do not be surprised if your partner doesn't immediately welcome and accept your changed behavior. Relationships don't start fresh every day; they have a history. Not only do men need to take responsibility for their behavior in a particular incident, they also need to be accountable for how past abuse has affected their partners' behavior today.

3. *Do the next right thing.* You probably know that Alcoholics Anonymous meetings are full of sayings such as "One day at a time." One of the more recent slogans is "We just need to do the next right thing." If you choose to do the next right thing for yourself and the woman you love, and you are certain that you are making a moral choice, then you will be the man you want to be.

Try it: loosen your grip. Let go of your need to control, and do the next right thing. A new world will open up for you.

chapter four

How Did I Get This Way?
—The Trap

"When I was about eleven years old I got slammed in the elbow with a baseball during a Little League game. God, it hurt! I dropped the bat and clutched my elbow and started to cry. Hanging on to my elbow was bad enough, but the crying was too much for my dad. He yelled from behind the fence, 'You're all right! Stop crying!' My mother got up from her chair and came toward the fence, but Dad told her to leave me alone. *He* didn't leave me alone, though—he kept shouting at me to stop crying and take it like a man. I made myself let go of my elbow and took my base. I stared at the ground, hoping my dad couldn't see under the bill of my helmet." Ron, who had been worried about thoughts of injuring his wife, told Randy this story during a counseling session.

Most of us can identify with Ron's story. We all remember times when we were shamed into trying to be more manly, even if we were only eleven years old. These efforts by our parents and coaches were effective in teaching us that boys don't cry, and they also made it difficult for us to express any kind of pain or fear without feeling like a loser.

Ron's family was typical in many ways. His mother worked half-time at the local library, and his father was a bookkeeper for a furniture factory. While his father rarely shouted and was never physically abusive, he made the major decisions in the family without much input from his wife. Ron had two sisters: Adele, two years younger, and Mary, three years older. Ron was the only boy.

"My dad didn't ignore Mary and Adele, but it was always clear that they were the girls and should do things with Mom," Ron recalled. "He would praise them for being pretty or getting good grades or for helping Mom. After dinner we'd leave the table, and he'd always tell them to help her clean up. I thought that's the way things were supposed to be."

Ron's father took him camping, participated in his Boy Scout activities, and helped him with school projects, but there was a price to pay for his attention. His dad was a demanding perfectionist, and Ron rarely did things up to his standards. His father would praise a B-plus on Mary's report card, but questioned why the same grade on Ron's report card wasn't an A. Adele wasn't reprimanded if she cried when she fell off the swing, but Ron couldn't remember a time when it was okay for him to cry.

"If I did something that he didn't like or that wasn't good enough, he would hiss at me, 'Control yourself! You've gotta control yourself to do your best!' But crying or showing fear was the worst thing I could do in his eyes." Ron paused as a memory washed over him. "Fear or crying only showed that I wasn't in control of myself and was acting like a girl. When he was really mad he'd make me feel bad by saying that Adele would make a better son than me."

Ron was pelted with these contradictory messages throughout his boyhood. On one side, his father tried to "turn him into a man" by shaming him and making him feel that nothing he did was ever good enough. Ron's father believed that bullying his son in this way would toughen him up. On the other side was the message that simply by being a male he was better than his sisters. The two messages combined to form an ugly threat: if you don't measure up, then you're weak, like a girl.

Ron isn't alone. From the moment we are born until our deaths, we are bombarded with messages about what it takes to be a man. As infants, we are bounced more and cuddled less than baby girls. Our mothers coo to us less, and our fathers tend to play more roughly with us. We get kicked off our parents' laps much sooner than our sisters do. As we get older, we are hit from all sides with advice, threats, and insinuations about how to measure up by parents, siblings, cousins, uncles, girlfriends, teachers, coaches, neighbors, other boys, television, songs, pro sports stars, movies, ads, video games . . . you get the idea.

Male Socialization

The process of "turning a boy into a man"—as if he wouldn't grow up to be a man on his own!—is called *male socialization*. Every society, now and in the past, socializes its children. Boys and girls are taught how to behave so that they can fit in with other people. A society functions smoothly when most of its members agree most of the time to follow certain rules and ways of behaving. Most of us pay our taxes, follow street signs, and dress and eat in ways that don't shock our neighbors. Socialization varies from one society to another. Westerners don't eat fried dog meat for dinner, for example, but such a meal would be acceptable in Korea or China, where people are socialized to use dogs as a source of food.

Socialization concerns itself with the needs of a *society*, not with the needs of the individuals who make up that society. Serious problems arise when the socialization process strips individuals of some of the abilities they need to function as well-adjusted human beings. This is what happened to Ron.

The male socialization process taught him

- to deny physical pain and emotional vulnerability
- to be powerful and in control at all times
- to be bigger, stronger, and smarter than girls
- to devalue anything that hinted at "girl" behavior

Many of these lessons focused on denying physical and emotional pain and maintaining control of himself and the situation around him. Expressing emotion was for mothers and sisters, and Ron learned to ignore his feelings. Eventually, Ron lost the ability to feel much at all except anger and frustration. He was unaware of the deep pool of shame and fear that made him worry constantly that he wouldn't measure up, wouldn't be successful, wouldn't be a "real man."

Ron quickly became conscious of that shame and fear when he lost his job as a regional manager during a downsizing at the grocery store chain he worked for. The loss of his job ate at Ron because he mistakenly believed that by working hard and contributing to the company's profitability he could avoid being laid off. In fact, Ron, who was consistently competitive and hardworking, had done everything right to keep his job. But his boss was told to lay off four employees, and he chose seniority as the easiest way to make the cuts. Although Ron had been there for eight years, some of the other managers had been there far longer.

At home, Ron struggled with the fact that he had lost his role as breadwinner. Leslie, his wife, tried to be supportive, but everything she said began to grate on Ron. He yelled at her that she was stupid when she brought up the idea of getting a job herself. He got even angrier when Leslie mentioned that he could seek the help of an employment counselor. Ron finally sought help from Randy when he recognized that he did not know how to behave without being abusive. "I'm just on the edge," he said carefully. "I almost slapped her the other night. I'm afraid I'm going to do something to her that I'll regret."

Losing his job did not cause Ron to be abusive, any more than drinking causes domestic violence. As long as he was employed and maintained control at home, Ron's world was fairly stable. But being laid off made him feel robbed of a job that was rightfully his. The loss of his job tilted the balance of control away from Ron and increased the stress from the hidden anger, fear, and shame that had gnawed at him since his boyhood socialization into manhood. As his control at work vanished, Ron felt a need to gain more control at home.

The "Act-Like-a-Man Box"

In his book *Men's Work*, sociologist and author Paul Kivel uses an exercise called the "Act-Like-a-Man Box" to depict the socialization process that boys endure. You can make a version of the box yourself: draw a square on a sheet of paper and list inside all the traits and characteristics you can think of that boys learn are desirable in men. When he was six or seven years old, Ron's box would have included words and phrases like *brave, tough, doesn't act like a girl, doesn't cry*. Until he was eight or nine, these were the words or suggestions Ron heard that described how men are supposed to act. As he grew older, Ron heard more messages. Most of them weren't very subtle. By the time he was a teenager, Ron's box would have added words like *fearless, independent, in control, strong, competitive, unemotional, stoic,* and *able to score*.

The last entry—"able to score"—was wishful thinking for some guys, but it was nonetheless a characteristic that was considered necessary to be a real man. From the teen years through the beginning of old age, men receive constant messages from other men and from popular culture that they are supposed to be able to get women to have sex with them.

When Ron first began counseling, his box had a few added terms.

fearless	stoic
tough	in control
in command	strong
brave	capable
independent	never cries
able to endure pain	unemotional
always ready for sex	invulnerable
rational	competitive
able to score	silent
provider	protector

The words in your box won't be identical to Ron's, of course, but they would have had the same underlying goal of "turning you into a man" when you were a boy. *Now that you are a man, the purpose of the words is to keep you inside the box.* You know the image of the ideal man, because you've heard the same messages Ron did. For the generation after World War II, he was made popular by the characters portrayed by John Wayne, such as cowboy, war hero, or submarine captain. The "real man" was the rugged individualist without permanent family ties, although he could always get a woman if he wanted one. Later, he was Superman, Rambo, Dirty Harry, and the Marlboro Man. Today some of his traditional roles remain popular, like cowboy and soldier, but the Man in the Box is also characterized by sports heroes, rap artists, and violent video game characters.

The words inside the box describe a warped male ideal. There's certainly nothing wrong with being *strong, tough, brave,* or *capable.* Instead, the problem with the words inside the box is that they severely limit a man's life. These "masculine" words restrict both experiences and emotions; they make life one-dimensional. Because they are so limiting, some boys and men get outside the box to live life more fully. A few of the terms that might describe them are listed on the left side of the box below.

nurturing	**fearless**	**stoic**
uncertain	**tough**	**in control**
emotional	**in command**	**strong**
artistic	**brave**	**capable**
vulnerable	**independent**	**never cries**
creative	**able to endure pain**	**unemotional**
sensitive	**always ready for sex**	**invulnerable**
loving	**rational**	**competitive**
dependent	**able to score**	**silent**
flexible	**provider**	**protector**

The boy or man who risks stepping outside the box by showing some of the characteristics listed at the left also risks being called names. You already know these names; you've heard them before. You usually don't say them unless you want to insult another man or perhaps tease him. Dare to step outside the box, and you will be belittled by all the terms commonly used to shame a man or boy who violates the male code the box describes. If, like Ron as a boy, your eleven-year-old son cries when he's struck on the elbow by a baseball during a Little League game, he'll be called names such as *sissy, fag, mama's boy, girl, wimp, crybaby, scared, queer, wuss*—the list might not be endless, but it's long. You may have called him some of these names yourself.

Kivel's point is unmistakable: if you want to be a man, you must stay inside the box and live according to the characteristics listed there. Because showing fear or emotion has traditionally been considered unmasculine in our society, any boy or man who displays such "weakness" is asking to be

nurturing	**fearless**	**stoic**	*wuss*
uncertain	**tough**	**in control**	*girl*
emotional	**in command**	**strong**	*sissy*
artistic	**brave**	**capable**	*fag*
vulnerable	**independent**	**never cries**	*wimp*
creative	**able to endure pain**	**unemotional**	*crybaby*
sensitive	**always ready for sex**	**invulnerable**	*scared*
loving	**rational**	**competitive**	*mama's boy*
dependent	**able to score**	**silent**	*queer*
flexible	**provider**	**protector**	*gay*

shamed back into the box. The words on the right side of the box above can twist a boy's guts until he feels physically ill. They can gnaw at his heart and erode his faith in himself. A deep and lasting injury is created through the process of male socialization that a man carries with him.

What happens to a boy who is called names like these? Too often, in addition to making him feel rotten, he is treated differently by his peers. The words at the bottom of the box below describe what happens to the boy who doesn't fit into the box.

nurturing	**fearless**	**stoic**	*wuss*
uncertain	**tough**	**in control**	*girl*
emotional	**in command**	**strong**	*sissy*
artistic	**brave**	**capable**	*fag*
vulnerable	**independent**	**never cries**	*wimp*
creative	**able to endure pain**	**unemotional**	*crybaby*
sensitive	**always ready for sex**	**invulnerable**	*scared*
loving	**rational**	**competitive**	*mama's boy*
dependent	**able to score**	**silent**	*queer*
flexible	**provider**	**protector**	*gay*

left out   beat up   picked on   chosen last
bullied   harassed   not invited

Anyone subjected to such treatment has to find some means of coping. Many of the men we see who have been convicted of domestic abuse harbor deep feelings of anger and resentment that they sometimes are not even aware of. Listed at the top of the box below are ways in which men typically respond or act out.

| depression | revenge | violence | isolation | avoidance |
| | substance abuse | | hypermasculinity | |

nurturing	**fearless**	**stoic**	*wuss*
uncertain	**tough**	**in control**	*girl*
emotional	**in command**	**strong**	*sissy*
artistic	**brave**	**capable**	*fag*
vulnerable	**independent**	**never cries**	*wimp*
creative	**able to endure pain**	**unemotional**	*crybaby*
sensitive	**always ready for sex**	**invulnerable**	*scared*
loving	**rational**	**competitive**	*mama's boy*
dependent	**able to score**	**silent**	*queer*
flexible	**provider**	**protector**	*gay*

left out   beat up   picked on   chosen last
bullied   harassed   not invited

Notice that the words on the right side of the box have something strikingly in common. They are primarily effeminate terms that convey a clear message: "Stop being feminine, start being masculine, and get the hell back in the box." This is the crux of male socialization, the male code: "act like a man."

We live up to the male code by fighting to prove toughness, engaging in high-risk behaviors to show fearlessness, and seeking sexual conquests to confirm our heterosexuality and sexual prowess. We become very aware of pecking order, whether we are keeping track of who caught the biggest fish or sank the most baskets or who's the best machinist/

attorney/salesman in our work group. Our socialization may prepare us for limited roles and success in society, but at a terrible price. The box does little to prepare us for intimate relationships. The box tells us to be in control, deny emotions, be invulnerable, and compete, while intimacy requires us to be respectful, emotionally engaged, vulnerable, and loving. As men, we long for companionship, security, and love, but we approach our intimate relationships with skills that lead to control, conflict, loneliness, and abuse.

We sacrifice half our humanity to reach the pinnacle of masculinity.

Just a Girl

Because this sacrifice requires that we devalue "feminine" characteristics, such as empathy, nurturing, and listening skills, we also have to devalue our wives and girlfriends. According to the myth of male superiority, they are, after all, just girls. Their devaluation is the logical outcome of traditional male socialization, which teaches boys that they are better and more important than girls. It also teaches boys that they need to control themselves and the situation around them. As Ron learned, this can be a formula for domestic abuse.

In counseling with Randy, Ron learned that his sense of self-worth hinged on his ability to be in control. He had learned his boyhood lessons well. He controlled his feelings. He rarely showed anger outwardly and was only occasionally affectionate with Leslie and their two children. For the most part his family went along with what he wanted, so he felt in control at home. As long as he worked hard, he believed he could control his work environment enough to protect his job. But the company downsizing was out of his control, and the depression and feelings of worthlessness that followed his layoff also seemed to be beyond his control. Ron found himself in a downward spiral, first lashing out at Leslie verbally, and finally worried that he might hit her.

Randy and Ron worked together to harness the best parts of Ron's strict self-discipline while helping him recognize and accept two practical truths: first, no man can be in total control of himself and his world all the time; second, not being in total control doesn't mean that the world will fly into pieces and the man will be exposed as being less than a man.

More important, Ron began to understand the root of his impulse to take out his feelings of shame and fear on Leslie by abusing her. Ron had been taught for years, both at home and in the world outside his home, that boys were better than girls and that women should comfort and support men. Above all, men should be in control. It never crossed Ron's mind to slug the manager who signed his pink slip, but his impulse to hit Leslie was very strong and seemed to come out of nowhere. Why? *Without consciously thinking about it, Ron believed Leslie was not as good as he was and deserved to bear the brunt of his shame, anger, and fear over losing his job.* Ron almost slipped into violence not because he lost his job, but because he had never been forced to consider his underlying beliefs about women. In his mind, it was Leslie's job to comfort and sustain him, and she wasn't measuring up to the task. Ron certainly wasn't to blame for an upbringing that stressed male control and superiority, but he *was* responsible for his behavior as an adult. To Ron's credit, he chose his love for his wife and family and began counseling with Randy rather than indulging his own fears and insecurities and blaming Leslie for his problems.

Not Everyone Gets the Flu

When the flu season arrives, many people sail through without being troubled by a single sniffle. Their muscles don't ache, they don't have a fever, and they can show up for work. Other people may suffer a few symptoms and feel under the weather for several days. But a few, exposed to the same germs, spend a miserable week in bed. In the same way, almost all boys in our society are exposed to the same sorts of trauma by male socialization, but they do not all grow up to be violent and abusive. Men like Ron lose their jobs every day, but not all of them turn to domestic violence. Why would Ron think of harming Leslie, while other men might accept their wives' support and encouragement? There is no clear answer to this question, other than the obvious fact that we are all different and respond in different ways to the same stimulus.

For boys who grow up with low self-esteem and shame, buying into the tenets of the Act-Like-a-Man Box props them up with a false sense of power, control, and security. Control and power over a woman can temporarily compensate for the feelings of powerlessness and shame they chronically experience in their life. Ron was susceptible to his father's bullying attempts to "turn him into a man," and he felt deeply shamed when he failed to live up to his father's expectations. Providing for his family was an expectation that Ron adopted from his father, and it was a nonnegotiable issue: either you made a comfortable living or you were less than a man. Other men who were socialized in similar ways might feel superior to women, and they probably feel rotten if they lose their jobs, but they never hit their wives. Being exposed to a "bug" doesn't mean you are doomed to suffer the flu, even if everyone around you gets sick.

Winning at Work, Losing at Home

The male socialization process almost always involves shaming or bullying boys while at the same time instilling the false belief of male superiority. Some boys are also encouraged to accept another false belief: that they are superior not only to girls, but to just about everyone else. Such distorted beliefs form the basis of *grandiosity,* that is, an inflated sense of confidence and self-worth.

- A middle school boy's baseball team loses by twelve runs, but his father tells him they were only having a bad day; the other team just got lucky. If the rest of his team had played as well as he did, they surely would have won.
- A fourth-grade boy is frequently in trouble at school. His report card grades are exclusively Cs and Ds. Yet his father beams with pride while watching him play basketball, proclaiming that his son is "All boy!" Both parents praise his academic efforts. His father tells him he doesn't have to suck up to his teacher (that is, behave in class) just to get better grades. His mother assures him, "We know you're smarter than those other kids. You just get bored in school, don't you?"
- A handsome, popular high school junior has one attractive girlfriend after another. He rarely finishes projects and chores he has promised to do. He is frequently teased by his father in a good-natured way. "You've got it made, son—the guys like you and the girls can't keep their hands off you! Remember, it's not what you do that counts so much as whether people like you."

The results of such distorted thinking aren't difficult to imagine. Boys like the ones in the examples above tend to grow into men who turn a blind eye to the realities of failure and who always think they are right, no matter what the situation. They tend to blame others—after all, they can't be at fault themselves—and think it is their right to be aggressive in controlling those around them. A grandiose man with an exaggerated sense of self-worth often has difficulty seeing himself and others realistically. He is offended when the world doesn't go his way, and he sometimes strikes back at perceived insults and injustices. That's what happened to Charlie's client, John.

John's dad was quite different from Ron's father. Ron was taught to control his emotions and do well in school, but his father never pushed him to excel in athletics or to take on the neighborhood boys. Nor did Ron receive the message that he was better than everyone else. John's father, in contrast, encouraged John to "stand up for himself" with other boys and not to let his girlfriend tell him what to do. John's dad told him that he should never let others "push him around," because that would only show that John was inferior, like a girl. John spent his boyhood swinging between grandiosity and shame, at times thinking he was the cock of the walk and at other times living in fear that he would be found to be weak and inferior.

"He always told me, 'Don't let them push you around. You're better than they are, and they need to know it.'" John related this boyhood training one evening in group.

"Who were 'they'?" asked Charlie. "Did he mean particular people, or just the world in general?"

John thought for a moment. "Well, not the whole world, but just about everyone I knew: other guys on the football team, my friends, even my teachers. He'd say that just because they knew a little more than I did didn't make them any better than me."

John strutted through high school. He antagonized his teachers, irritated his coaches, and kept only those friends who would go along with him. From the outside he appeared successful: he had a pretty girlfriend, guys to hang out with, and was the football team's star running back. Often he got away with misbehavior because of his status on the team— the coach would persuade teachers to look the other way when John was late, didn't turn in homework, or challenged them. As a result, John didn't learn much about being accountable for his actions. After high school he worked construction for several years. He saved as much money as he could and eventually started his own roofing business. By the time he was thirty-four, John had a regular crew of ten people, and when weather permitted he hired subcontractors. His aggressive, bullying style made few friends, but his projects were completed on time and his customers were usually satisfied. John shrugged off the workers' dislike as the cost of doing business. "I don't go to work to have guys *like* me," he explained. "I go to make sure they do the job right. Sometimes I have to be a little hard on them."

Because John knew only one way of dealing with people, he carried this attitude home with him. He frequently told Jessica, his longtime girlfriend, how to improve her performance at work and how she should do things around their home. Jessica tried to follow his directions, and when she didn't, John could easily intimidate her by raising his voice and shaking her slightly. He always insisted that he had her best interests at heart and only wanted to help her be as successful as possible. One evening, after John criticized an important decision Jessica had made at work, she finally blew up at him. John didn't see her resentment as a result of his interference on a subject he knew little about. Instead, he thought Jessica was acting disrespectfully. This was one thing John couldn't stand. He began pushing Jessica across their crowded living room, and when she shouted at him to stop, he responded by slapping her repeatedly. The abuse stopped when Jessica lost her balance and struck her head on the sharp corner of a glass coffee table. John was instantly apologetic, although he thought the injury was her own fault, and Jessica assured him she was okay. When she could get to her cell phone alone, Jessica called the police.

Charlie recalls that John was stunned not only by Jessica's "disrespect," but also by what John saw as her betrayal by calling the police after he assaulted her. His exaggerated belief in his own self-worth had been challenged, but it was never seriously shaken.

"Eventually John learned to stop shaking and pushing Jessica, and he even stopped raising his voice to scare her," Charlie says. "But he never made the connection between his boyhood experiences and his violent behavior. He just couldn't let go of the idea that Jessica should obey him because he knew better than she did, regardless of the subject. And he certainly never figured out that his violence grew out of an overwhelming fear that her standing up to him would make him less of a man."

In other words, John remained trapped in a confining box from his boyhood that dictated not only how he should behave, but how others should behave as well. Jessica eventually grew tired of life within the trap, and she left John less than a year after he pushed her into the coffee table.

Escaping the Trap

The way out of controlling and abusing others is by embracing our full humanity. We need to blast the box of false masculinity into outer space. We are not islands or rocks unto ourselves, entitled to control others for our benefit. We are humans who may have had half our humanity squashed in the name of manliness. Fight back! We can reclaim our compassion, love, and respect for others. We can have feelings, admit mistakes, communicate, and let go of control, while at the same time maintaining our masculinity. In fact, a real man is a man of integrity, compassion, respect, and courage. Not just the kind of weekend courage and compassion that let him climb a ladder to build a house for Habitat for Humanity, but the kind of steady, daily courage it takes to step outside the box, withstand the potential mockery, and do the right thing: love and respect his partner without control and abuse.

No man is ever to blame for his upbringing and the male socialization process that he experienced as a boy, but he is always responsible for his behavior as an adult.

chapter five

The Dynamics of Domestic Abuse

T om was thirty when he met Sally. She was playful, classy, attractive, and twenty-three. She seemed like the perfect wife. Because she was the fulfillment of his fantasies, Tom was a little surprised when Sally was attracted to him. In his experience, women like Sally usually went for the guys with more education, more polish. But Sally liked the fact that Tom was a practical, down-to-earth man who had made a career for himself. As a real estate agent, Tom made more than a hundred thousand dollars a year, although he came from a poorer background than hers and hadn't gone to college.

When Tom first met Sally's parents, he had been impressed but nervous. Their house looked like it had been decorated for a movie—no pets, no dust, no mess. In fact, it didn't look as if anyone lived there. Sally's father was an attorney; her mother volunteered at the Art Institute. Like her mother, Sally had a degree in art history. Tom wasn't sure her parents would welcome a son-in-law without a college education, but that did not stop him from asking Sally to marry him. Their lavish wedding—Tom was shocked at how much her parents spent—was attended mostly by the bride's wide circle of family and friends. Tom invited his parents, his brother, and several people he knew from work.

For the first year of their marriage, nothing seemed wrong. Sally was loving and attentive. Although their house never looked like her parents' home and they ate out a lot because Sally rarely cooked, Tom enjoyed his new role as husband. But he also wanted a family. Sally didn't want to give up her part-time job at the museum to have children until she was at least twenty-eight, but Tom pressured her until she agreed. Their sons, Jason and Aaron, were born only two years apart. After the boys were born, Tom assumed that Sally would quit her job and give her full attention to her family.

In spite of her misgivings about having children before she was ready, Sally loved her sons. She took them to the zoo and the park and playgroups with other young mothers. Yet Tom found himself more and more irritated with her because she wasn't changing some of her other behaviors. She still liked shopping with her mother and always seemed to have new clothes—too many, from Tom's point of view, and from time to time he gave her little talks on budgeting. There were other problems. With two boys under the age of four they didn't go out to eat as much as they had before, and Tom liked dinner ready when he got home. His mother always had a home-cooked meal ready when his father came home in the evening. The problem with Sally, Tom mused, wasn't just that she didn't cook meals from scratch; often, she didn't cook anything at all. So he gave her another of his lectures on the role of a wife, and when she objected, he told her she'd better do what he said because she wasn't really that attractive and no one else would have her. Tom knew this wasn't true, but Sally's expression told him she partially believed what he said.

Tom still saw himself as an easygoing guy, but coming home to an empty house really bothered him. A few times, he found a note on the refrigerator saying, "Home at seven." One night Sally came home with the boys at eight o'clock, chattering about how the boys enjoyed the storytelling at the library. Ten minutes later Sally's mother called. For the next half hour Sally was on the phone describing every detail of her day, leaving Tom, tired and hungry, to watch Aaron and Jason.

Tom increasingly saw Sally as careless and unloving. In his head he knew that she was almost always home in the evenings and still loved him and wanted to please him, but deep down he felt he no longer came first. His occasional lectures about buying clothes and cooking turned into sermons—about housekeeping, about spending less money, about how she should spend her time, about being a good mother and wife. He said that a married woman should be home in the evenings with her husband. Sally defended herself. "I spend an evening at Mom and Dad's house less than once a week. They like to see the boys. And besides, you're at that club at least one night a week playing cards."

Tom simply responded, "That's different." In an effort to make peace, Sally tried to be home every single evening and talk with her mother only when Tom wasn't around. Things got a little better. But Tom kept his eyes open and he brooded, a man on the lookout for further misbehaviors.

One cold Tuesday in November Tom came home early to a dark and empty house. He rustled through the refrigerator looking for something for dinner, gave up, got a bottle of beer instead, and flipped on the TV to watch the news. At 7:30, Sally finally arrived home. She hugged him and said, "I thought you wouldn't be home until eight. Isn't this the night you play basketball?"

"It got cancelled."

"I wish you'd called. I was just at Mom's."

"You're always at your mom's," Tom said.

Sally could see that Tom was tense, and she said, "I'm going to put the boys to bed." An hour later, she returned to the living room. "I'm sorry, Tom," she said as she cuddled up beside him. "I'm sorry you came home and we weren't here."

There was a silence. Tom said, "You spend too much time at her house."

"Tom, I try so hard to—"

"You don't try hard enough," he said, standing up and starting to pace across the room. "I work ten, sometimes twelve hours a day, and you can't even be here when I get home. You don't have dinner ready. Christ, there wasn't a thing to eat in the fridge."

"If you'd just called Mom's—"

Tom interrupted her. "Your mom. Your mom," he said angrily. "It's always about your *mother.*" He picked up his beer bottle and threw it against the brick fireplace. It shattered on the hearth.

"Tom!" Sally exclaimed. She jumped up and moved quickly into the hallway.

"Where the hell are you going?"

"I think the boys and I should leave until you cool down."

Tom stopped her in the hall. She tried to walk past him, but he grabbed her by the shoulders and slammed her against the wall. He brought his face close to hers and shouted, "Where are you going? To *Mom's?*"

"Let go of me," she screamed.

Tom took a step backward and slapped her hard across the face. "You're not going anywhere."

They stared at each other in silence, both shocked at what he had done. Tom stepped away from her and wordlessly returned to the living room. On a rerun of *ER,* doctors tended to another deluge of injured and bloody patients. In the kitchen, Sally quietly called 911.

The police arrived fifteen minutes later. When they asked Tom what happened, he told them that she was never home, that she couldn't cook a decent meal, and that she spent money as if he'd won the lottery. "At least I didn't hit her," he concluded.

The cop looked at him. "Yeah? So how'd she get a bloody lip?"

"I'd never hit a woman," Tom said. "I just slapped her."

The cop shook his head. "You're going to have to come with us, sir."

Tom spent the night in jail, and the next day the court issued an order saying that Tom couldn't see Sally or be on their property. As soon as he was released, Tom bought Sally three dozen roses and drove to their house. When she didn't answer the door, he left them on the front porch. He also left her a note suggesting that they meet at a mutual friend's. He returned a few hours later and waited another hour, parked in his own driveway. When she didn't show up, he finally threw the roses in the garbage.

Eventually, Tom was convicted of domestic violence. He was allowed to go home, but he was ordered to attend a domestic abuse treatment group as part of his probation. Although he was still angry, Tom remained calm on the outside. Sally tried to do everything he wanted, but she was strained and distant. Mostly, things were tense, and it felt like they were just going through the motions of having a relationship.

He couldn't believe it when he learned that the group met every Thursday night for six months. On his first night, there were twelve guys in the room. At the beginning of the meeting, Charlie said they'd have a check-in during which each man would say what he had done to bring him to the group. The first guy, Chuck, said he had pushed his girlfriend, Sarah, down on the bed and choked her. Rich had slammed the car door on his wife as she was attempting to leave during a loud argument. When Tom's turn came, he said that he really didn't need to be in the group because his wife completely neglected him. He thought *she* should be in a group to teach her how to be a good wife.

Charlie intervened. "In this group, Tom, we don't talk about her. We could spend all day long talking about how awful you think she is and get nowhere. We need to talk about ourselves and how we can change."

Tom was infuriated and became still angrier when another group member said to him, "After a while you'll see that you're always responsible for your behavior no matter what anybody else does. Once you change your attitude, things will get a lot better at your house."

It took five long months of painful self-exploration in weekly group sessions, but Tom eventually did realize that he had been controlling and abusive. One evening, he asked Sally if they could talk. "I'm so sorry, I'm so terribly sorry," he said to her. "I know things haven't been very good around here, but I still want us to be married. I think I'm learning how to be a better husband."

Sally, who had listened over the months as he first ranted about the group and then slowly began to change his behavior, hugged him and wept. "Of course I want us to stay married," she answered. "I always wanted to make a life with you."

The Process of Domestic Abuse

Tom was a decent, hardworking man who wanted the best for his family. But as his hurt and anger and insecurity overwhelmed him, Tom's thinking became distorted. He truly believed he deserved Sally's constant attention. In his view, she intentionally failed to meet his needs. She seemed to spend far more time on Aaron and Jason than on him. Worse, he magnified his hurt and anger by dwelling on her failure to properly care for him. He blamed her for his bad feelings. Eventually, Tom overreacted to the shortcomings he perceived in Sally's behavior by becoming abusive.

Tom had fallen into a pattern of domestic abuse that could destroy his wife and family. Men like Tom who are stuck in this repeated pattern, or process, act out abusively without much awareness of their underlying feelings or thoughts. Over time, they are similar to the alcoholic who drinks every day. Just as drinking regularly seems normal to the alcoholic, the abusive man comes to believe that controlling his partner is the only way of relating to her.

This pattern involves feeling, thinking, acting, and reacting. The Dynamics of Domestic Abuse Wheel illustrated below shows how abusive behavior flows outward from a man's deep-seated fears (center of the wheel), his sense of entitlement

The Dynamics of Domestic Abuse Wheel

(first ring), and his need for power and control over his partner (third ring). The eight types of abuse shown on the wheel (fourth ring) are used to obtain gratification (fifth ring), or in other words, a man uses abuse tactics to get what he wants from his partner. The final ring shows the tactics he can use to cover up his abusive actions and their effects on his partner.

Here is a summary of the six rings of the wheel.

Fear: Being afraid to feel and appropriately express
my hurt, fear, and shame
Entitlement: The distorted belief that I have the right
to get what I want
Power and control: Getting what I want by deliberately
imposing my will on my partner to gain power
over her
Abuse tactics: Eight common tactics to control my
partner
Gratification: The achievement of my wants and
desires through abuse
Cover-up: Hiding the abuse from myself or
others through denial, blame, minimization,
justification, and honeymooning

Fear

No fear is the mantra of masculinity. We see it posted on men's vehicles and printed on T-shirts. As men we aren't supposed to be controlled by our feelings, especially fear. Consequently, most men are not going to admit to themselves, much less others, that they fear that their partners may leave them, shame them, smother them, or simply not care for them. We place these insecurities and fears at the center of the wheel because they lie deep inside a man's core, submerged by years of denial. Rather than feeling the fear, he often just converts fears into anger. The anger can then justify his beliefs and energize his actions. Like Tom, some men develop distorted ways of thinking to protect themselves from having to face these fears.

Here are some symptoms that tell us we are experiencing fear. Which of these do you find yourself experiencing when you are with your partner?

_____ *I feel tense and agitated.*
_____ *I get a burning sensation in my stomach.*
_____ *My heart beats really fast.*
_____ *I clench my jaw or fists.*
_____ *I begin pacing and have trouble sitting still.*

Entitlement

Entitlement is an attitude that says, "I've got rights—the right to get what I want, the right to have things be the way I want them, the right to tell other people what to do." It includes the belief that "I have the right to be controlling and abusive to get people to do what I want them to. If they are hurt by what I do, it's not my fault. I really have no choice." Entitlement is a narcissistic point of view that assumes the world centers around the individual and should meet his needs.

It's easy to feel that we're entitled. Our socialization as boys encourages us to believe that as males we should get what we want from women. Tom spent years watching his mother serve his father a home-cooked meal when he got home from work, so it isn't surprising that he expected the same treatment from Sally. Men who believe they are entitled to make the world fit them don't begin their adult lives as abusive monsters. In fact, they may not even be aware of their belief in entitlement. A *belief* may not be a conscious thought, such as a deliberate belief in a religious doctrine. Sometimes our beliefs remain hidden from us, but they direct our actions nonetheless. Thus, for some men, entitlement is a hidden, unacknowledged belief. It seems to be the nature of things—entitlement benefits them, yes, but it's also part of a natural world order in which men get their needs met first. Often their sense of entitlement becomes so habitual that they lose sight of the fact that other people, especially their partners, suffer because of their gains, and they become increasingly entrenched and aggressive in maintaining their top-dog roles.

In addition to their sense of entitlement, men try to get others to meet their needs because they don't know how to care for themselves. Tom had no close friends, he didn't confide in his family, and he didn't know how to enjoy his own company. In his job as a real estate agent he could be friendly and socially responsive, but at home he needed Sally's unswerving devotion and attention to feel complete. Sally's life, on the other hand, was filled with friends and family. She enjoyed visiting them, both alone and with the boys. To her, loving Tom didn't mean being with him every available moment. But because Tom felt lonely when she was at her mother's or with her friends, he told her she was a poor excuse for a mother and wife and that she spent too much time away from home.

Tom's sense of entitlement also led him to the dangerous belief that he was above the law. He assumed that he was entitled to speak with Sally in spite of the fact that the court had issued a no-contact order.

Patriarchy, a special form of entitlement often practiced by men who abuse their partners, is the belief that the man should be the head of household. The word *patriarch* has two roots. *Patria,* which means family, comes from the word for father *(pater),* and *arch* is a word ending that means to be first or to rule. So the patriarch is the ruling male in a family. He's in charge; he's the boss and he makes the decisions, or, if the woman has some say, he'll make the final decision.

Many of us grew up in patriarchal homes. Our fathers

made most of the major decisions about how to spend family money, where we lived, and whether our mothers worked outside the home. Our mothers' decisions were often about less important matters such as decorating or food. Patriarchy worked poorly for many of our parents, especially our mothers. They may have looked as if they appreciated their husbands as protector-provider, but in fact they were often resentful. Because if Dad made the decisions, Mom didn't have the one thing that people want most: control of her own life.

Today, patriarchy is being challenged. Remarkable changes have occurred in our society over the past forty years in how we view other people, especially those whom we see as different from ourselves. We are more aware of discrimination at work and in our schools. We have come to believe in due process in hiring and firing, and we expect the protection of the legal system to ensure equal rights. In short, we believe in fairness in a way that no previous generation has.

Unfortunately, many men, like Tom, believe in fairness in the workplace but not at home. Tom lectured Sally about how she spent money. He felt justified in chiding her about her poor performance as a wife and mother. He even took his age (seven years older than Sally) as a reason to treat her like an irresponsible child. In short, Tom's outdated patriarchal worldview led him to treat Sally without the fairness and respect she deserved as his life partner. The key term here is *partner.* Sally isn't Tom's child or his live-in cook; she is half of their husband-and-wife team.

Spend a couple of minutes thinking about how you use entitlement, especially patriarchy, to get what you want.

___ *I make all or most of the major decisions in our home without negotiation.*

___ *I decide how money, including my partner's earnings, should be spent.*

_____ *I have strongly influenced my partner to get, keep, or quit a job.*

_____ *I decide what's best for the children in spite of my partner's wishes.*

_____ *I should not be questioned when I have expressed my opinion or made a decision.*

_____ *I make sure that the entire family sees my needs as a top priority.*

_____ *I am the head of the family because that's how things are supposed to be.*

_____ *I require that my partner be subordinate to me.*

_____ *I usually tell my partner what she can and cannot do.*

_____ *I have convinced my family that my ideas and values are best for everybody.*

Power and control

In the dynamics of domestic abuse, control is the act of imposing your will on your partner to fulfill your own sense of entitlement. Control almost always involves the use of emotional or physical abuse to give you power over your partner. Power lets you meet your needs at the expense of hurting your partner. As part of an ugly cycle, abuse always carries with it the unspoken threat of further abuse as a means of control.

When we first tell the men in our groups that domestic abuse stems from the desire to control their partners, they don't believe us. They roll their eyes and shake their heads and argue. Almost all of them blame the woman for provoking their violence. They say they were angry or drunk. But when we ask them to tell the group what they did that resulted in their arrest, this is what they say:

Jason: Mary wanted to leave to see her sister. I wanted her to spend the evening with me, so I grabbed the keys away from her and she cut her hand.

But I'm supposed to be the head of the household . . .

You may believe that men are ordained or created by God to be leaders in their homes. If you accept the patriarchal concept of headship, then it may be difficult for you to confront the most self-serving of your patriarchal attitudes, beliefs, and behaviors. No matter how strongly you feel about these ideas, there is no justification for the use of violence, abuse, and control to carry out these beliefs. Any leadership role in the family must be conducted with respect and love. A man can't justify his abusive behavior by claiming that his partner was disobedient or insubordinate. We are always responsible for our actions and reactions. In fact, abusive behavior isn't headship, but tyranny disguised as leadership. When you use violence, abuse, or manipulative control tactics as the head of the house, you resort to being a controller, not a leader. Do you rely on your religious beliefs to support your emotional need for control in your intimate relationships? If so, then you are at continuing risk of inflicting abusive behavior on your partner. But if you truly believe you are honoring a divine social arrangement, your headship role needs to embrace respect, love, compassion, and empowering leadership.

Bill: Amanda wouldn't stop yelling and calling me names during an argument. I grabbed her shirt and told her to stop, but she wouldn't. Then I grabbed her by the throat and slapped her.

Jack: I came home and caught Dolly talking to this guy she works with. I didn't want her talking to him, so I grabbed the phone away from her. When she started arguing with me I hit her.

Marvin: Mindy didn't want to listen to me. She turned her head away, and I yelled at her in the loudest voice I've ever used that she needed to listen to me and look at me when I talked to her. I held her chin hard and made her look at me while I talked.

As we look at their stories, we see that each act of violence began as an act of control. Jason controlled Mary by using force so she couldn't leave. Bill choked and slapped Amanda to control how she spoke to him. Jack's message to Dolly was that she wasn't to talk with other men—and he hit her to make her fearful enough of him that she wouldn't do it again. Marvin wanted Mindy's undivided attention. When she looked away, he used his superior strength to force her to look at him.

Tom tried to control Sally in a variety of ways. He pushed her to have children and wanted her to quit her job after they were born. He told her she was too unattractive to expect anyone else to be interested in her, even though he knew this wasn't true. He restricted her behavior by trying to isolate her from her family and make her stay home. He frequently let her know that she had not met his wishes. He threw a beer bottle, a physically threatening message of how upset he was that she didn't submit to his will. He blocked Sally in the hallway, controlling her by stopping her from leaving. Finally, he slapped her across the face, an action clearly meant to frighten and demean Sally and to reinforce his insistence that she must change her behavior and stay at home to serve him and care for his needs. Lastly, he blamed *her* for his abusive behavior to support his belief that she, not he, was the one who needed to change.

From what we know of Tom and Sally's life, it doesn't appear that she spent too much time with her mother. But even if she did—and here's a significant point about control— Tom wasn't entitled to control her life and punish her for not complying with his wishes.

Abuse tactics

In our groups we first help the men see that their desire for control leads to violence. Often they have misconceptions about what *violence* really means. They understand that men who physically injure their wives or girlfriends should be arrested. But when they look at their own reasons for arrest, they believe the police and courts overreacted. "All I did was push her a little," they'll say. Too often, they minimize their behavior and don't see it as abusive.

Sometimes it takes the men even longer to recognize that abuse includes behavior that does not involve physical violence. "I only shouted and slammed the door," they'll say. "I never *touched* her!" In fact, abusive behavior includes tactics such as isolating your partner from her family and friends or trying to destroy her self-esteem.

The eight abuse tactics shown on the Dynamics of Domestic Abuse Wheel are only general categories; we can't list every single type of tactic that a man might use. If you don't see exactly what you've done on the list, don't think you're off the hook. We want you to think of similar ways you may have injured or tried to control your partner.

Physical abuse. When you use your size or strength to push, grab, choke, or strike your partner, you are being physically abusive. Physical abuse—any act that physically harms or injures your partner—is domestic violence. Other actions, such as holding her down or blocking her way, are also types of physical abuse even if they don't involve obvious violence.

When we discuss Tom's story in our groups, most of the men immediately identify slapping Sally as an act of physical abuse. Occasionally someone will agree with Tom's comment to the policeman and say, "Well, at least he didn't hit her." Some of the men who have been in the group for a while will challenge him, noting that a slap is a hit. Eventually someone will point out that blocking Sally in the hallway is still another act of abuse because Tom uses his superior strength to control Sally's actions.

Physical abuse is serious for three reasons:

First, physical abuse creates fear and destroys trust. The bond of the relationship is broken or seriously damaged.

Second, physical abuse can too easily result in injury. Domestic violence is the single largest cause of injury to women age fifteen to forty-four, according to the American College of Emergency Physicians in 2003. By contrast, it is the seventh most common cause of injury to men.

Third, physical abuse makes the relationship unequal because the man can usually inflict far greater injury than the woman can. Even if your partner hits you back—or hits first—it is unlikely that she can injure you as much as you can injure her.

Emotional abuse. Certainly men need to avoid physical abuse above all else. But emotional abuse (calling her a bitch, telling her she's stupid, criticizing or humiliating her) is hurtful, too. Each time you use an emotional abuse tactic against your partner you injure her sense of self-worth. In fact, when we speak at shelters to women who have been the victims of domestic abuse, they tell us that it is the emotional abuse that *lasts*—it's the abuse that erodes their self-esteem and makes them feel nervous in their own homes. An emotionally abused woman is easy to control because her self-esteem is low. She will question her own values, ideas, and feelings while deferring to yours.

If you have used any of these strategies—and you probably have used more than one—you have emotionally abused your partner:

___ *Calling her demeaning names such as "idiot" or "bitch"*
___ *Swearing at her*
___ *Using sarcasm at her expense*
___ *Interrupting her so she can't finish her statements*
___ *Negatively comparing her to others*
___ *Criticizing or belittling her appearance, housekeeping, or cooking*
___ *Making her feel stupid or crazy*
___ *Giving her the silent treatment or withholding affection*
___ *Belittling her ideas, arguments, or values*
___ *Humiliating or embarrassing her in front of others*
___ *Telling her she's a bad mother*

Coercive sex. Coercive sex occurs any time you force your partner to be sexual when she doesn't want to or in ways she doesn't want to. Sexual abuse may include waking your partner for sex or making her say or do things that cause her pain or embarrassment. Coercive sex also includes episodes of forced sex in any form. Forced sex is rape. In our groups, most guys don't want to talk about this shameful tactic. They want to believe that their partners always consent or choose to have sex. But when they are asked to describe in detail what happened, the men realize that their partners had sex not out of desire but out of fear. Coercive sex tactics don't build intimacy. They punch holes in your partner's sacred self, leaving her feeling violated. These coercive sexual tactics are only a sample:

___ *Criticizing her sexual performance*
___ *Yelling at her for refusing sex*
___ *Putting her on a schedule for sex*

_____ *Giving her the silent treatment if she doesn't have sex*
_____ *Forcing yourself on her despite her pleadings to stop*
_____ *Manipulating her into acts she finds inappropriate or uncomfortable*
_____ *Bringing pornography or sex toys into your sex life without her consent*

Intimidation and threats. This tactic allows you to create fear in your partner. Men can create fear loudly, by yelling and destroying property, or they can do it quietly, by stalking a woman or threatening to harm her or her children. Acts of intimidation and threats keep your partner fearful and on edge. She never knows what you might do next. Consequently, she may walk on eggshells while attempting to please you or calm you down. Steve, a forty-two-year-old bricklayer, explained in group, "I haven't hit her for years. All I have to do is give her that 'look' and she shuts up." This tactic is powerful because it creates fear, confusion, and uncertainty in your partner. Any of the following actions—and there are many more—could make your partner feel threatened and intimidated:

_____ *Yelling and screaming at her*
_____ *Threatening to leave her*
_____ *Destroying personal or household property*
_____ *Slamming doors*
_____ *Threatening to call child protective services*
_____ *Driving recklessly when she is in the car*
_____ *Acting out of control or dangerous*
_____ *Threatening to hurt the kids or pets*
_____ *Displaying weapons during or after arguments*
_____ *Threatening to disclose intimate details of her life to others*
_____ *Staring or scowling angrily at her*
_____ *Stalking her*

_____ *Showing up against her wishes when she is at work or with friends or family*

Isolation. When you interfere with your partner's ability to form or keep relationships with others you are using isolation tactics. People are easier to control when they feel unloved and cut off from others. Oppressive systems such as religious cults use this tactic because it is effective in keeping new converts in line. Isolation makes your partner more dependent on you. You may be threatened by her relationships with others, particularly when deep down you know that you don't treat her very well. You are probably afraid that others may support, love, and respect her in ways you don't. To drive her away from her family, friends, neighbors, or co-workers, in your mind, is to steer her into a more dependent relationship with you. When discussing their isolation tactics, men in our groups frequently explain, "Her friends aren't good for her," "Her family is pretty shady," or "If she's at home I don't have to worry about her." These statements are almost always excuses for using isolation tactics that are intended to decrease the man's fear of being deserted or replaced.

Here are some specific examples of isolation tactics:

_____ *Criticizing her family and friends*
_____ *Disabling the car so she can't leave*
_____ *Monitoring and interfering with her e-mail, phone calls, and mail*
_____ *Being unavailable to care for the children so she can't go out*
_____ *Belittling her hobbies and interests*
_____ *Preventing her from developing relationships with work friends*
_____ *Logging her mileage on the car to keep track of her comings and goings*

_____ *Interrogating her about where she is going, where she has been, and with whom*

Using other people. This is the process of influencing other people to support your control over your partner or to get them to actively reject or criticize her. For example, in a group session, Harry admitted that he had convinced their minister that his wife had a drinking problem so that she wouldn't be allowed to sing in the choir anymore. Aaron's strategy was similar: he told his wife's doctor that she was taking more than the prescribed dose of a pain medication, and the doctor stopped prescribing it. Using your partner's children to punish her or to influence her decisions can cause great pain. Mona told Charlie in a collateral session that she moved back in with her partner during a separation because her kids became uncontrollable. "Their father turned them against me for breaking up the family. I couldn't take their abuse and threats to never see me again, so I moved back." Using others to control your partner is abusive because it turns people she depends on for support and love against her. She feels pain and isolation. You feel gratified and in control.

These are a few examples of the tactic of using other people to harm your partner:

_____ *Persuading her family that she has mental health problems*
_____ *Manipulating the children to turn against your partner, their mother*
_____ *Getting others to feel sorry for you by misinforming them*
_____ *Telling your partner negative things that others didn't actually say*
_____ *Misleading professionals and the court about your abuse and control*

____ *Getting others to spy on your partner to get information*
____ *Being rude to her family, friends, or co-workers to keep them away from her*

Economic abuse. Money is power. If you control the money at your house, then you have power and privilege and your partner is economically dependent. Economic dependence doesn't necessarily mean that your partner is deprived. Some men like to keep their wives or girlfriends in a golden cage. The woman inside may have everything she needs or wants that money can buy, but she must always ask her partner for the money. Other men deliberately deprive their partners of money. These men know that money can help buy independence, and they want to make sure that their partners can't leave them.

These are several specific examples of economic abuse:

____ *Preventing your partner from getting a job*
____ *Denying her access to family income*
____ *Lying about the status of money*
____ *Making her ask you for money*
____ *Depriving her of fun money while giving it to yourself*
____ *Inducing guilt over her purchases while justifying yours*
____ *Insisting that she give you her money*
____ *Pretending that money is tight in order to control her spending*

Male privilege. Male privilege is the belief that men have certain rights and privileges simply because they're men. Tom believed that he had the right be out in the evening for a game of basketball or playing poker at a friend's house, but that Sally didn't. She should stay home and care for the children. He believed that she should cook for him. He dictated not only *that* she should cook but also *how* she should cook: he wanted home-cooked meals from scratch. The idea that he might cook for himself never seems to have occurred to him.

An abusive man uses male privilege as a deliberate tactic when he defines the roles of men and women to secure his power, control, and special status as a man. This tactic works best when he can rely on some outside authority to prove that as the man, he should be in charge. He may use history, religion, or social tradition to convince his partner that her job is to serve and support him. By using male privilege tactics, a man can declare himself king of the castle without reason or merit.

Eli, a forty-seven-year-old professor of theology, announced during his intake assessment with Randy that he was the head of the household "because the Bible says so." He learned later in counseling that he clung defensively to such a doctrine not because he was trying to follow God's will, but because it gave him power and control and allowed him to lord it over his wife, Jillian. Justifying what he saw as the biblical doctrine of male privilege was easier for Eli than admitting that he used his religious beliefs to get his needs met. The tactic of male privilege safeguards you from feeling powerless and from the work of negotiation; you haul out the false rules to get what you want when you want it.

Here are some other examples of male privilege. How many of these beliefs do you try to put into practice?

___ *Housekeeping is almost always women's work.*
___ *Cooking, except on the grill outside, is women's work.*
___ *Child care is primarily women's work because women are naturally suited to it.*
___ *Women are responsible for maintaining family ties.*
___ *Men only need to talk or share when they are ready or when they feel it is necessary.*

____ *Women should serve men by providing their time,*
attention, and care.

____ *Men have the right to determine appropriate behavior*
for men and women.

____ *Men get to choose which family obligations they will be*
responsible for.

Gratification

Achieving control through abuse allows a man to feel a fleeting gratification. He feels entitled to this gratification because he feels entitled to getting his way or getting what he wants. For a brief time he has forced his partner to comply with his wishes, and as a result he temporarily feels less angry and anxious. He feels empowered because he thinks he is in control. Tom felt empowered with each successive step of his abuse of Sally on the night of his arrest. Arguing with her, throwing the beer bottle against the fireplace, and blocking her in the hallway all made him feel strong and in control. But his elation vanished as soon as he hit his wife. He saw the fear and disbelief on her face and knew immediately that he had broken a trust that he might not be able to mend.

You may not wish to have total control over your partner, but you likely have used abusive tactics to get your partner to stop or start certain behaviors. You may want her to stop yelling, stop spending, or stop leaving. You stop her with abusive tactics. You may want your partner to start cleaning, start loving, or start parenting more. By using control tactics, you manipulate her into starting the actions you desire. For a brief time—a week, a day, a minute—you are satisfied that you have gotten what you wanted. But the feeling of gratification never lasts. Like an alcoholic, you will soon need another shot of control to feel the same gratification again. Worse, your desire for gratification will follow the law of diminishing returns. In the same way that a cocaine addict needs increasingly large amounts of cocaine to feel a rush, your abuse will need to escalate so that you can continue to get what you want.

Cover-up

Once you have achieved gratification through power and control over your partner, you are likely to try to persuade both yourself and her that the abuse did not happen. Cover-up strategies are intended to let you hide or disguise your abusive actions so you don't have to face the painful and shameful reality of your behavior and its consequences.

Denial is the effort to convince the abuser and others that an abusive behavior didn't happen. Al, a member of one of Charlie's groups, made the classic statement: "I'm not in denial. It just didn't happen." The "it" that didn't happen was Al's dragging his girlfriend down a public sidewalk while hitting her in the face. Three separate witnesses gave similar accounts of the incident. Other men in our groups have insisted that their wives deliberately injured themselves to frame them, or that they never yell, despite actively raising their voices in group to others. When looking at shameful behavior is too painful, denial is an incredibly powerful shield against having to admit guilt or accountability.

Blame occurs when an abusive man makes other people or conditions responsible for his behavior. Blame is the mirror that deflects a man's responsibility for his actions onto his partner, alcohol, work stress, or his temper. It is always much easier for a man to blame others for abusive or violent behavior than to take ownership for his abusive need to control his partner. Too often, we hear "She started it," "She knows exactly how to make me mad," "She bruises easily," or "She's too sensitive." There are an endless number of ways to blame someone else for your wrongdoing. Blame also gets professionals, friends, family, and children to see your partner, not you, as the problem.

Minimization tries to make light of a situation and make a problem seem smaller than it really is. You may try to persuade your partner that you only pushed her a little bit, when in fact you hit her in the stomach. When the police arrive at your door after neighbors call them to complain of screaming and shouting, you'll assure the officers that you were only having a minor argument—nothing serious. Men who minimize often talk about their domestic abuse in group by saying "All couples fight" or "It's not like I hit her" or "It really wasn't that bad" or "She's just making a big deal out of this." An abusive man minimizes so he doesn't have to face the painful and sometimes shocking reality of how serious and destructive his abuse is. Ironically, the smaller you make the problem, the bigger it becomes. Your partner knows what you did to her, and her anger, fear, and resentment will only increase if you tell her she is imagining things.

Justification lets a man rationalize his abusive and controlling behavior. He will try to justify his abusive actions to convince others that his behavior is somehow normal given the circumstances and his partner. Phil, a prosperous business owner, tried to justify his economic and emotional abuse of his wife by explaining to the other members in Randy's group that the Bible required women to obey their husbands. He lamented how the women's movement has created undue and unnatural power for women. "Women have laws they can use to frame us," Phil argued. "We're all good men, just trying to maintain our place in society and in our families."

Another common justification is that the woman is unreliable and unstable, and that the man has no choice but to control her behavior for her own good. Some men justify abusive behavior by insisting that they had to defend themselves against an aggressive partner. For men who rely on justification to cover up their responsibility, abuse and violence are an understandable and justifiable response to women's insubordination and failure to appreciate traditionally accepted standards of male and female behavior. When you use justification, you hide behind a cloak of rationality rather than make yourself accountable for your actions.

Repair and honeymooning: *Repair* is a man's attempt to quickly fix the relationship after an abusive episode so he can feel good about himself and in control again as fast as possible. If you have abused your partner you may tell her you're sorry, you won't do it again, you'll go to counseling, you'll talk to the priest, you'll stop drinking. You will probably make all sorts of promises to win her back. Repair is a cover-up strategy because its promises and apologies are false. If the repair works, and you persuade your partner to trust you or give you another chance, then you enter the honeymoon phase.

Honeymooning does the same as courting behavior in the early part of a relationship. When you first started to see your partner, you were on your best behavior. You tried to do and say all the right things to make a good impression and secure her love and devotion. Now you try the same strategy again. You tell her she's pretty, that she's the love of your life, that you'd be nowhere without her. You go to work, talk to the priest, start counseling, and fix the leaky sink. You admit your wrongdoings and send flowers, cards, or chocolates. All this activity cultivates your partner's hope for the future. But repair and honeymooning are like taking aspirin to get rid of a hangover—they work until you start drinking again. Repair and honeymooning may work in the short run, but until you stop your abusive, controlling behavior you will be trapped in the cycle of domestic abuse and your partner's renewed hopes will be shattered.

The Cycle Continues

In the movie *Sleeping with the Enemy,* Laura Bernie (played by Julia Roberts) marries Martin, an attractive and successful

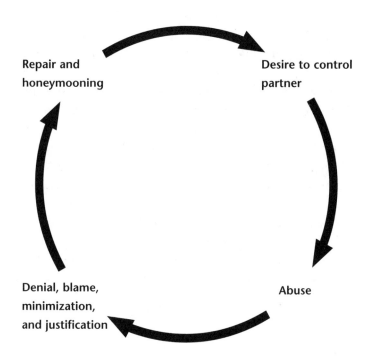

Cycle of Abuse in Relationships

man. Although superficially caring and respectful, Martin is in fact a compulsive, controlling, and violent man. In a pivotal scene, Martin convinces himself that Laura has been having an affair. He backhands her, and when she falls down, he kicks her. In a feigned act of remorse, Martin leaves and returns with a negligee—a cruel gift for a woman whose injuries are still fresh and who by this time has sex with him out of fear rather than love. He says to her, "I'm sorry we quarreled," minimizing the truth of what happened in an effort to make himself look good. Martin looks sorry, but Laura and the audience are not fooled. Everyone knows that unless Laura escapes, it is only a matter of time before Martin is again physically violent with her.

Your partner may suffer the same fate if you continue to be primarily motivated by securing your relationship through control and abuse. (See "Cycle of Abuse in Relationships" diagram on page 83.) If you are not ready for the hard work of recovery, then the honeymoon will end and the dynamics of abuse will unavoidably start up again. You will continue to bury your fears and transform all feelings into anger. You will cling to entitlement and other distorted thinking, and the need for power and control will slowly grow. Using abusive and controlling tactics is a seductive pattern because for a while, it works. It's addictive. You can get what you want with a look or a slam of your fist.

Changing your behavior is hard. It takes commitment and it takes self-understanding, which can be gained by getting to know the kind of man you are.

chapter six

What Kind of Man Am I?

You've learned about the cycle that domestic abuse typically follows. Now we invite you to take a closer look at yourself. As you read Tom's story you may have said to yourself, "Well, I'd never do that" or "That's not like me at all!" We chose Tom as a representative example, but of course the nature and severity of men's abusive behavior vary, just as men themselves do. Because the personalities of such men vary, what they fear, what triggers them, and what control tactics they use tend to be different as well.

We'd like you to complete the following questionnaire, which identifies six types of abusive personalities. Categorizing yourself as one personality or another is less important than being able to pick out and understand your characteristic behavior, especially your control tactics and what triggers them. Once you begin to identify your triggers (that is, what starts your abusive behavior), you will be better equipped to tackle the challenge of responding to the triggers and the fears they represent in a nonabusive way.

We urge you to take the time to read each item slowly and consider your response carefully. Don't simply skim through the items and answer quickly, or worse, not answer at all. Answer as honestly as you can. There are no right or wrong answers. We've included directions and a brief analysis of each personality type below. For more information, please see our Web site at www.menscenter.org.

Change is a journey, and some of the suggested changes require intensive long-term counseling, while other suggestions can be applied to your life immediately. Identifying your beliefs and expectations about women and relationships can happen fairly quickly. Actually *changing* those beliefs and expectations may take a little longer. However, you may need to work awhile with a trained therapist to learn how to manage your core fears, that is, those most deeply hidden fears that underlie your abusive behavior.

What Kind of Man Am I?

Self-Assessment

This questionnaire can help you understand your own personality style, triggers for abusive behaviors, and self-management strategies. It was developed with the help of a group of men in a domestic abuse intervention program. While it can be an effective tool for men who have engaged in abusive behaviors toward their partners, *this assessment will not identify a man as abusive, rate the risk of a man's becoming abusive, or rate an abusive man's probability of continued abuse.*

Instructions

Read each numbered item in the left column. Next to it, use the scale of 0–4 to rate the degree to which it describes you. For example, if the item is not like you at all, circle 0. If it is very much like you, circle 4. If it describes you somewhat, rate it as 1, 2, or 3. Please respond honestly to each item. Skipping items will lower the effectiveness of this assessment. When you are done, use the key on pages 89–90 for scoring.

	Not Like Me			Very Much Like Me	
1. I worry that my partner will leave me.	0	1	2	3	4
2. I demand my partner's undying attention.	0	1	2	3	4
3. My partner complains that I interfere with her social relationships.	0	1	2	3	4
4. People say I don't talk much and I'm hard to get to know.	0	1	2	3	4
5. People have told me that I'm paranoid.	0	1	2	3	4
6. My partner has complained that I don't talk very much.	0	1	2	3	4
7. I hate it when my partner surprises me with a change in plans.	0	1	2	3	4
8. It drives me crazy to wait for dinner when my partner said we'd eat at six.	0	1	2	3	4
9. I prefer to do things around the house rather than being with people in the house.	0	1	2	3	4
10. When people don't do what I want, I get angry and let them know how I feel.	0	1	2	3	4
11. There are lots of crazy and dangerous people in the world and you have to watch out.	0	1	2	3	4
12. I like to be in control of things and in charge of people: it's safe that way.	0	1	2	3	4
13. It makes me uncomfortable when my partner gets emotional.	0	1	2	3	4
14. People have told me that I'm too uptight.	0	1	2	3	4
15. It upsets me when my partner seems to want to be with other people more than me.	0	1	2	3	4

	Not Like Me			Very Much Like Me
16. My partner has complained that I'm a perfectionist.	0	1	2	3	4
17. My partner doesn't understand how important I am.	0	1	2	3	4
18. My partner keeps things from me.	0	1	2	3	4
19. I long for my partner's undying attention.	0	1	2	3	4
20. I have been in trouble with the law.	0	1	2	3	4
21. Whether I'm in a relationship or not, I feel lonely a lot of the time.	0	1	2	3	4
22. The home is a happier place to be when children are orderly and obedient.	0	1	2	3	4
23. Sometimes I feel really great and other times I feel crummy, and most of it is my partner's fault.	0	1	2	3	4
24. I've gotten into fights and had to use violence to protect myself.	0	1	2	3	4
25. I'm always suspicious of people's motives.	0	1	2	3	4
26. It upsets me that my partner can't seem to be organized.	0	1	2	3	4
27. When I'm out with my partner, it feels good to see other men looking at her.	0	1	2	3	4
28. You shouldn't trust other people; they'll just take advantage of you.	0	1	2	3	4
29. I sometimes think that people are talking about me behind my back.	0	1	2	3	4
30. When I'm angry with my partner, I shut her out as a way of showing her how I feel.	0	1	2	3	4

What Kind of Man Am I?

Scoring Key

Instructions

1. Record your answers under the six headings shown below and on next page. Start with the "Don't Leave Me" group, writing your answers to items 1, 3, 15, 19, and 21 in the "Your score" column. (For example, if you circled a "2" for item 1 in the assessment, write "2" in the "Your score" column after item 1.) Total your score under that heading, then repeat for the other five groups.

2. Under which two groups did you get the highest scores? When you have identified them, read the descriptions of those two personality styles in this chapter. You may see yourself in either one or both of the descriptions. If your scores don't clearly point to one or two personality types, read the other types as well as "There's Nothing Wrong with Me" to learn more about yourself.

"Don't Leave Me"
Items 1, 3, 15, 19, 21

Item #	Your score
1	
3	
15	
19	
21	
Total score	

"Put That Away"
Items 7, 14, 16, 22, 26

Item #	Your score
7	
14	
16	
22	
26	
Total score	

"It's Got to Be Me"
Items 2, 8, 17, 23, 27

Item #	Your score
2	
8	
17	
23	
27	
Total score	

"Leave Me Alone"
Items 4, 6, 9, 13, 30

Item #	Your score
4	
6	
9	
13	
30	
Total score	

"Don't Mess with Me"
Items 10, 12, 20, 24, 28

Item #	Your score
10	
12	
20	
24	
28	
Total score	

"They're Out to Get Me"
Items 5, 11, 18, 25, 29

Item #	Your score
5	
11	
18	
25	
29	
Total score	

Understanding Your Pattern of Abusive Behavior

Now that you have identified your type, let's see what else you can learn about yourself. We'd like you to remember three things as you read the descriptions that follow.

First, your scores may not place you neatly in a single personality type. Read all the descriptions, even the ones in which you have only one or two points, because you may still recognize some of your own behaviors and attitudes.

Second, some questionnaires provide a range of scores in an attempt to tell you how much you fit into a particular personality type. This questionnaire is not intended to do that. You need to look at your various scores and identify those that point to a particular personality type.

Third, we've explained the most common personality types, but we can't provide examples to fit everyone. Let's say that one of the men prevents his partner from attending a night class. Okay, going to a night class may be the last thing your partner would want to do. But if you have ever stopped her from doing something else, such as joining the church choir, taking off for a night with her women friends, taking two-step lessons, or joining the renters' association in your apartment building, then you have behaved in a similar way to the guy who stopped his partner from attending a night class. The details may be different, but the basic controlling behavior is the same.

For each personality type we suggest ways to overcome the weaknesses that get you in trouble. In subsequent chapters, we provide you with more strategies to help with your core fears, triggers, and tendency to control your partner.

"Don't Leave Me"

Bill describes his girlfriend, Amanda, as someone who blows hot and cold, sometimes loving and at other times insensitive. He thinks she spends too much time with other people and not enough with him. Sometimes he angrily confronts her about where she has been, what she has done, and who she has talked to. In response, Amanda withdraws, and Bill pursues her, demanding that she talk. On occasion, she locks herself in the bedroom, and Bill pounds on the door until she opens it. When he's upset, he checks her cell phone and e-mail logs.

Instead of seeing his own insecurities and fears as contributing to his behavior, Bill blames Amanda. "Well, she can't be trusted," he'll say, or "She's flirtatious" or "She's always late." Bill sees his behavior (pounding on doors and checking her calls) as normal reactions to *her* behavior. *He never understood that Amanda's "ups and downs" were actually the result of his own mood swings.* Amanda tried to maintain a sense of balance in the relationship, but eventually she lost her trust in and love for Bill. She adopted survival tactics to work her way out of a relationship she found oppressive and abusive. She moved out one day when he was at work.

Core fear and purpose of control. If Bill's story sounds familiar and you scored highest on this personality type, you often approach intimate relationships with desperation because you struggle with insecurity and fear of abandonment. You control your partner so she won't leave you. She probably feels smothered and pulls away from you. You believe that increased control will secure the relationship and that coercion will mold her into the right lover. As the abuse escalates, your partner is apt to become increasingly unhappy and the relationship more unstable. In extreme cases, these cyclical phases in the relationship can escalate into serious abuse or homicide, especially during times of abrupt separation.

Triggers and tactics. You tend to act out abusively when your partner comes home late, wants to go out with a friend, or doesn't give you the attention you think you deserve. You may get upset when she wants more independence, such as getting a job or having her own checking account. If she spends time with the kids, you may get upset because you believe she should be taking care of you. Seeing her talk with another man at a party worries you: without any evidence, you begin to imagine they are planning an affair. To make yourself feel more secure, you use power and control tactics to prevent your partner from leaving or to punish her for perceived injustices, slights, or not taking care of you. You want to know where she's going, who she talks to, and when she'll be home. Your typical tactics involve economic control and isolating her from her family and friends. These tactics make her socially and economically dependent on you, which helps you feel more loved and secure.

Your partner's experience. Your partner is initially attracted by how much you dote on her. She is flattered by your attention, personal sacrifices, and emotional engagement. But after a few months, she begins to feel suffocated. Loving you is getting more difficult because you demand more and more of her time and attention and offer less and less in return. Your neediness and jealousy wear her down. She feels more trapped and afraid as your control tactics increase in intensity.

What you need to work on. Your controlling behavior is directly linked to your inability to hold your own hand. In other words, you emotionally lean on your partner to feel stable, secure, and loved. To stop controlling her will make you feel as if your relationship is becoming unstable, insecure, and unloving. But as you increase your ability to care for yourself, you will be able to calm yourself when you feel agitated by your triggers. Challenge your beliefs about women and relationships to develop more appropriate and healthy expectations. Until you can learn to support, trust, and respect yourself, you will remain desperate and likely at risk of abusiveness in intimate relationships.

Key points of the "Don't Leave Me" personality
- *Core fears:* Abandonment, rejection, or being left out in relationships
- *Purpose of control tactics:* To keep his partner trapped and dependent
- *Triggers:* Perception that his partner is withdrawing or not meeting his needs for constant reassurance
- *Preferred tactics:* Isolation, economic control
- *Partner's chief complaint:* "He's insecure and jealous; I can't breathe"
- *Self-management tasks:* Developing realistic and appropriate expectations about women and relationships; learning greater independence

"Put That Away"

Conrad, an engineer, is the keeper of the rules and regulations at his house. His obsession with detail makes him a good engineer, but he can be a difficult co-worker. His family tolerates his controlling behavior, but they don't like it. He tried posting the house rules in the hallway, but there was such a revolt that he resorted to regularly assigning tasks for everyone, including his wife, Stacy. Conrad wants companionship but fears being overwhelmed by the messy emotions of intimacy. He controls to minimize his anxiety by making his partner, relationships, and world predictable. In his view, the ends do justify the means. In other words, if he needs to demand a clean and orderly home in order to secure a calm and predictable existence, then he will do so. He sometimes uses threats and anger (shouting, pounding on tables, slamming doors) as intimidation tactics to get his family to comply with his demands. His four children and Stacy experience him as distant at best, and demanding and controlling at worst.

Core fear and purpose of control. A high score on this personality type strongly suggests that your core fear is that your life, particularly your personal relationships, will get out of control and that you will be buried under an avalanche of confused, disordered emotions. You want companionship, but you fear intimacy. You control to minimize your anxiety by making your partner, relationships, and world predictable. If your partner cannot meet your unreasonably high standards, you may eventually discard her as damaged goods and move on. Your risk of abuse and control escalates when you can't establish some perceived order in life, whether that is a clean and paid-off house, a happy family, or divorce with joint custody.

Triggers and tactics. You are triggered by disorder, unpredictability, and emotionality. You expect rules to be followed and order to be maintained. A minor issue for others, such as a dirty car or an unexpected change in plans, is a major trigger for you. Consequently, when rules bend or change occurs, you rage and control. You become anxious, and then controlling, when your partner doesn't clean, cook, parent, or love you according to your rules. Your control tactics may include the use of male privilege to demand obedience to these rules. You will use emotional abuse to berate insubordinate family members, and even physical abuse to get your point across. Your family ends up constantly anxious and worried about keeping things perfect because they know that you will make them suffer for imperfection.

Your partner's experience. Your partner was drawn to you because she thought you would take care of her. Your ability to be organized, disciplined, and responsible made her feel safe. She found comfort and security in your dependability and attention to details. At some point in your relationship, she stopped seeing your perfectionism as an asset, and now she realizes she's in a no-win situation. She can try to go along with your demands, knowing that she will rarely satisfy you, or she can ignore them, knowing that the consequences of ignoring you might be worse than trying but failing to please you. She may have accepted your judgment that she can't do anything right, which will lower her self-esteem and chances for happiness and interdependence in a more balanced relationship.

What you need to work on. You will be a happier man and a more respectful partner if you let go of your attempt to control your life by controlling your partner. Part of letting go will be you accepting that controlling your partner and family is impossible as well as undesirable. You can make a better life if you become more aware of your rigid beliefs about intimacy, family, and households and if you modify those beliefs to include the inevitable ebbs and flows of life. You will need to distinguish preferences from necessities, recognizing that some things are important and other things really don't matter. In order to achieve intimacy in relationships you will need to reprioritize; loving and respectful relationships are a higher priority than a clean, predictable, emotionless existence. If you ultimately decide that order and predictability are more important to you than being involved in a relationship, then you owe it to any future partners to remain uncommitted.

Key points of the "Put That Away" personality
- *Core fears:* Disorder, losing control, being suffocated by intimacy
- *Purpose of control tactics:* To manage fears by keeping emotions and physical surroundings tidy and predictable
- *Triggers:* Messiness, insubordination, displays of emotion, unexpected change
- *Preferred tactics:* Male privilege, anger, emotional and/or physical abuse

- *Partner's chief complaint:* "He's a control freak and a perfectionist; I never do anything right"
- *Self-management tasks:* Decreasing his need to control his partner by increasing his flexibility and tolerance for disorder; increasing his ability to open himself to the emotions and ups and downs of intimacy

"It's Got to Be Me"

Gordie is self-absorbed; others sometimes experience him as a man who believes the world should center on him. He likes to be in relationships with people who make him feel special. Gordie likes to align himself with powerful and respected individuals and institutions as a way of making himself feel important. He tends to view relationships in terms of what others can do for him. Gordie had the opportunity to go to college, but he dropped out during his first year. Now he relies on his family name to prop himself up, despite having only a sales position in the well-known car dealership started by his father and uncles. Being "one of the guys" is not enough—Gordie wants the biggest house, the fastest car, the most expensive home theater system, the flashiest wife. Patricia, Gordie's attractive wife, is a successful patent attorney. He depends on Patricia to support their upper-middle-class lifestyle and demands her unwavering support and attention. Gordie insists on being affirmed, validated, and respected as the competent, handsome, knowledgeable decision-maker of the house. When she met him, Patricia liked Gordie's charm and good humor. Now she is tired of catering to his ego and fearful of his abuse.

Core fear and purpose of control. If you scored highest on the personality type like Gordie's, your core fear is being shamed, ignored, criticized, or made to feel small and insignificant. Your controlling behavior is often designed to keep your relationship in the romantic or fantasy stage of love. This is the most rewarding stage of love for you because your partner sees you as charming, likable, attractive, larger than life, and most important, worthy of pleasing. You don't want to experience yourself or the relationship in terms of reality—that is, after your chosen princess discovers that her prince has a few warts. When she discovers your faults, she may pull back and no longer provide you with the attention you crave. You are abusive to make her understand that you are entitled to this form of devotion. The escalation of control and abuse will be proportionate to how much you depend on your partner for your self-esteem. When you need her as a mirror or a prop, then you may go to great lengths to keep her unconditionally supportive, affirming, and subordinate.

Triggers and tactics. Your core fear of feeling shame or inferiority makes you susceptible to many triggers. Perceived slights or suggestions that you are not as important as you think you are cause you to turn to your partner for affirmation and support. When these triggers occur outside your relationship, you feel entitled to her immediate attention. Triggers that occur inside the relationship, such as when you believe your partner is disloyal or critical or when she questions or challenges you, are likely to cause anger and disgust with her. You can be socially adept outside the family, but you are likely to use emotional abuse tactics such as mind games at home. For example, you may complain when your partner spends money "we don't have" on the kids' school clothes. She reduces the money she spends. Later you complain that the kids look ragged and that she is a neglectful mother because she doesn't send the kids to school in decent clothes.

You may try to belittle her by telling her she isn't very

good in bed, isn't much fun to be around, isn't very smart, or simply isn't good enough. This tactic of emotional abuse erodes her self-esteem and sets her up to try harder to please you. As a result, you feel better about yourself (because you're better than she is) and she gives you even more attention and affirmation.

Finally, you rely on your beliefs about male privilege and entitlement to support your demands. When your usual tactics begin to fail, you may use intimidation and threats; these will likely escalate to physical abuse if your partner does not play her assigned role.

Your partner's experience. At first, your partner found you engaging, charming, and amusing. She enjoyed being with you and enjoyed having you show her off. Over time, she wanted to establish a more mature relationship, but you blocked her. Eventually she feels disgusted with your refusal to grow up and fearful of your abuse if she doesn't continue to support and flatter you. Your emotional abuse is wearing her down, and she is tired of feeling invisible while having to hold up a mirror for you. She wants love, care, and a mutual relationship; she doesn't want to polish your ego for the rest of her life. If she is able to provide for herself financially, she may consider leaving.

What you need to work on. You need to see your partner as a separate person who has needs and emotions rather than simply using her as a supportive, affirming crutch to help you manage feelings of shame and inferiority. Rather than depending on her to prop you up, you need to work on developing a more realistic view of yourself. Part of this realistic view will be an appropriate level of grounded, authentic self-respect. This genuine self-respect—not grandiosity—will come from finding, and facing, the causes that lie behind you never feeling good enough. The change from grandiosity to a realistic perception of yourself will be painful and difficult; it will also be a positive, life-changing experience for you.

> *Key points of the "It's Got to Be Me" personality*
> * *Core fears:* Shame, criticism, being ignored or made to feel small
> * *Purpose of control tactics:* To get his partner to validate, compliment, and affirm him
> * *Triggers:* Feeling shamed, ignored, slighted, or neglected
> * *Preferred tactics:* Emotional abuse, including criticism, belittling, and mind games; demanding constant attention and affirmation
> * *Partner's chief complaint:* "He's self-centered and arrogant; my job is to make him look and feel good"
> * *Self-management tasks:* See his partner as a person with needs and feelings rather than as a tool to prop up his shaky ego

"Leave Me Alone"

Stan works as a machinist in a tool and die shop. In his free time, he builds and races ORV dune buggies. He has a few friends who share his interests, but Stan knows little about them because they rarely talk about anything personal. Mostly, Stan enjoys time alone in his garage listening to music and working on his buggies. He becomes upset when his wife, Marilyn, criticizes him for all the time and money he spends on his hobby, especially because she doesn't even appreciate the fact that he is beginning to win some races at the regional sand drags. Stan doesn't express his anger very often. He swallows his angry and resentful feelings for weeks, sometimes months, until a trigger situation causes him to explode. He may ignore Marilyn for weeks when she complains that he should help out with the kids in the evening.

But some evening, after he has spent all day at work looking forward to uninterrupted solitude rebuilding a dune buggy engine, he'll suddenly express the bottled-up anger when Marilyn makes the same complaint one more time. When this happens, Stan yells and often throws whatever is closest to him. Days will pass before he even speaks to her. Stan uses alcohol and occasionally marijuana to calm himself down. He enjoys sex with Marilyn but thinks her need to snuggle and chat afterward is a waste of time.

Core fear and purpose of control. If you are like Stan, your core fear is being swallowed up by emotions (your own or your partner's) or intimacy. You experience any emotion as dangerous, whether it is anger or love, because you fear being swept away and losing yourself. Your control tactics are designed to keep your partner at a safe distance and to avoid any conflict or demand that requires emotional involvement, communication, or negotiation. You avoid her not only to sidestep conflict but also to leave yourself time and energy for what brings you enjoyment, your hobbies.

Triggers and tactics. Predictably, you respond to two related triggers. First, you strike back at demands for emotional involvement, whether these are intimate moments with your partner or angry confrontations. Because you avoid anger, you tend to blow up at inappropriate times. Second, you react decisively to any attempt to deprive you of the solitude you need to pursue your own interests. These major triggers are related because they both ask you to transfer time and effort away from yourself and your interests to your partner.

Sometimes you use control tactics preemptively to control your partner and thus decrease the chance of her demanding your attention and involvement. Withdrawal and silence are your preferred tactics. If those don't work, you can intimidate your partner by yelling or throwing things to shut down communication. You may threaten divorce to get your partner to back down from her needs for a more involved relationship. Because you find satisfaction and enjoyment in things rather than people, you may be selfish with money as well as time. Consequently, you may fund your hobbies while ignoring your partner's or family's needs. You are typically unmoved by your partner's social activities as long as they don't interfere with your schedule.

You usually feel that your partner is too needy, too emotional, and just too demanding. As a result, you tend to have a higher risk of abuse when she desires more out of the relationship than you do. However, you have an ability to detach and move on from relationships that aren't working or that have become too much trouble for you. As a result, you have the lowest risk of any of the personality types for acting violently when you are going through a separation or divorce.

Your partner's experience. Your partner was initially attracted by your emotional steadiness. She felt safe knowing that you weren't overly dependent on her, and she seemed comfortable with your independence. Over time, your partner began experiencing you as emotionally aloof, detached, and often uncaring. If she has family and friends to support her, she may be able to tolerate your refusal to be intimate with her. If she lacks people around her, she will suffer extreme loneliness as well as anger, resentment, and frustration in her relationship with you. She worries about how little attention you pay to your children, and she may be angry about you neglecting them.

What you need to work on. You need to work on seeing your partner as a person who has legitimate needs for intimacy. You need to give up the control tactics that make you feel safe and begin to deal with the uncomfortable emotions that arise when you are intimately involved with her. When approaching conflict, you need to remain emotionally and physically available, rather than retreating and engaging in withdrawal tactics. In other words, you need to develop more realistic beliefs about intimacy and conflict.

Key points of the "Leave Me Alone" personality
- *Core fears:* Emotions and intimacy; being swallowed up or smothered in relationships
- *Purpose of control tactics:* To avoid intimacy and emotion and to shut down arguments
- *Triggers:* Demands for communication or emotional involvement, particularly when those demands interfere with his own activities
- *Preferred tactics:* Silence, withdrawal, intimidation
- *Partner's chief complaint:* "He's more interested in his work and hobbies than me; I don't know why he got married"
- *Self-management tasks:* Opening up to intimacy and conflict while managing the emotions that will surface; spending less time, energy, and money on solitary activities and more on relationships

"Don't Mess with Me"

Stony's hostile, violent behavior makes holding a job difficult for him; currently he works as a security guard. His childhood was spent in an abusive, violent home, and he was in foster care before he was a teenager. He was in trouble for aggressive and unlawful behavior both at school and at home. Eventually Stony was expelled for assaulting a teacher, but he did manage to finish high school in alternative education. Stony has been married twice; he physically abused both his wives and cheated on them as well. Stony often calls Carol, his girlfriend, ugly, degrading names. He was recently arrested for domestic violence for hitting Carol twice with a closed fist. She required several stitches. This was not the first time that Carol has needed medical attention. Stony doesn't consider himself to be abusive; he insists that Carol is a "crazy psycho."

Core fear and purpose of control. If you scored highest on this personality type, then you probably know you are an aggressive or intimidating man who uses abuse or power to get his way. Your behavior reflects your core fear: you are afraid of being dominated or feeling powerless. You only feel safe when you are in total control. In your world, a person is usually an aggressor or a victim, and you refuse to be a victim. You use control tactics to make certain that your partner is subservient, gratifies your needs, and doesn't try to take advantage of you or tell you what to do.

Triggers and tactics. You are easily triggered because you experience your partner's needs and wishes as betrayals or, at best, interruptions to getting your own way. In fact, you see your partner not as a *partner,* but as an object for your gratification. If she doesn't gratify or please you, then you can become abusive and violent. You can be very possessive, not allowing your partner a life outside of your relationship.

You may use abuse and violence to calm yourself. For you, being calm is the same as feeling powerful. You get a rush of power and a sense of calmness from intimidating, threatening, and using violence. You avoid violence only when it won't give you the control you seek. In fact, you are quick to leave a relationship to get someone "better," that is, someone you can control more completely. If a woman leaves you, you are likely to use abuse and violence to punish and harass her for leaving. Your partner soon learns that she suffers a high risk of violence with you. You may use weapons and seriously injure your partner.

Your partner's experience. In the beginning, your partner was attracted to your charm and outspokenness. She found you adventurous, fearless, and a little dangerous. She may have taken you on as a project to reform or a man she could settle down. Eventually, this project turned into a nightmare. Her family and friends probably do not know about the abuse she endures because you have been careful to isolate her. She lives in constant fear of your moods and violent responses. If she stays with you too long, your physical and verbal assaults may permanently damage her sense of self-worth. She also hesitates to leave because she knows you will punish her severely if she tries.

What you need to work on. For you, more than for any of the other personality types, it is essential to learn accountability in order to change. Changing yourself to keep a relationship together or to make another person feel better isn't big on your radar screen. You may consider personal change (sometimes temporary) when you tire of the legal and social consequences of your violence. Meanwhile, you are apt to continue your abusive behavior until you can begin seeing others as human beings deserving of respect rather than control. You need to learn to take responsibility for yourself and to be accountable for your actions, rather than blame everyone else for your problems. Life won't get easier and relationships won't work until you become more accountable and more human.

Key points of the "Don't Mess with Me" personality
- *Core fears:* Being powerless or dominated
- *Purpose of control tactics:* To get his partner to be subordinate and compliant and to force her to gratify his needs
- *Triggers:* His partner's needs, desires, or insubordination
- *Preferred tactics:* Threats and intimidation that escalate rapidly to physical violence
- *Partner's chief complaint:* "He's controlling, aggressive, mean, and violent"
- *Self-management tasks:* Seeing his partner as a person rather than an object; increasing accountability; decreasing violence, aggression, and blaming of others

"They're Out to Get Me"

Tyrone owns his own accounting and tax preparation business. He does as much of the work as he can because he doesn't trust that others can do it right or at all. He uses the Internet as little as possible because he worries that his files will be hacked into. He also mistrusts his girlfriend, Ann. In spite of her assurances that she is committed to their relationship and the absence of any evidence that she sees other men, Tyrone believes Ann cheats on him. On occasion he has checked her cell phone and e-mail records, and sometimes he calls her to make sure she is where she said she would be. Ann doesn't like being checked up on, and she and Tyrone quarrel frequently. He has thrown her down on a few occasions during intense arguments about her spending habits or her family. Tyrone likes the idea of having a girlfriend, but he sometimes wonders why he bothers because "you just can't trust women."

Core fear and purpose of control. Tyrone experiences deep feelings of distrust. He is suspicious of his partner's motives and doubts her truthfulness. If you scored highest on this personality type, then your core fears are betrayal and the pain of betrayal. To prevent the betrayal that you are certain is coming, you are drawn to control tactics that allow you to monitor and regulate your partner's activities. Sometimes you recognize that your thinking is "crazy," and you hold yourself back from examining her behavior. Other times, your distorted thinking takes over and you accuse her of things you later realize she couldn't or wouldn't ever do.

Triggers and tactics. Your most obvious trigger is a perceived betrayal. In fact, you are at risk of incorrectly reading intentions and motives into your partner's behavior. Ideally, you would isolate her from any contact with other people so you wouldn't have to worry about the threat of her leaving for another man. Instead, you watch who she sees and when, where, and for how long she sees them. You feel a bit more secure if you can maintain financial control in your relationship. If your partner has access to her own money, you fear she'll become too independent and wind up leaving you. When your suspicions are triggered, you can get very angry and emotional. You rely on verbal abuse as you self-righteously get your point across in an argument. Because you distrust your partner, you may intimidate her into stopping behavior she enjoys, such as going out with her friends in the evening. Finally, you may turn to physical violence in an escalated attempt to punish unacceptable behavior. You justify your abusive actions as "necessary, given the circumstances." These circumstances can broaden to include believing that your partner's family, friends, and co-workers have teamed up against you.

Your partner's experience. At the beginning of your relationship your partner may have been flattered by you always checking up on her, interpreting it as care and concern. She tried to quiet your fears and suspicions by constantly reassuring you of her loyalty and giving you detailed accounts of her activities. She began to withdraw from you when she realized you were suspicious and mistrustful no matter what she did or said. Now she tries to conceal information from you because she knows innocent actions can trigger your suspicions and abuse. If she is not financially dependent on you she will eventually grow tired of your lack of trust and move on.

What you need to work on. You need to work on trusting others, particularly your partner. This will make you feel very vulnerable, particularly in relationships where you have been angry and distrustful. Because she fears more anger, hurt, and self-righteous accusations, your partner may not want to let you back into her life. So the difficult task lies in trusting *yourself* to be trusting and understanding despite how she or others may respond. When you trust yourself, you can be trusting without becoming controlling or abusive. Ultimately, you will need to redefine intimacy to include vulnerability and times of insecurity and instability.

> *Key points of the "They're Out to Get Me" personality*
> - *Core fears:* Betrayal, emotional pain
> - *Purpose of control tactics:* To gain security in relationships, while punishing his partner for betrayals
> - *Triggers:* Any hint of betrayal, disloyalty, or unfaithfulness
> - *Preferred tactics:* Controlling his partner's social and financial life through spying and intimidation
> - *Partner's chief complaint:* "No matter what I do or say, he's always suspicious; I'm tired of his constant criticisms"
> - *Self-management tasks:* Tolerating vulnerability in relationships and learning to trust his partner

"There's Nothing Wrong with Me"

John works hard and is proud that he can provide his family with a comfortable living. He learned this value from his father, who stressed to John that a man should protect and be in charge of his family. John's mother cared for the family and was always available; she was never physically abused by her husband. John recalls being told often to stop crying, and he was spanked much more than his sister. The spankings stopped around the age of eleven, when he learned to make himself stop crying when he was punished. John loves his wife, April, and their three daughters; in fact, he enjoys being seen as a "family man." Nevertheless, he is easily overwhelmed by their persistent desires for a strong emotional relationship with him. He wants April to quietly take charge of their home life. John gets angry and confrontational when April presses him for more involvement. He is often intimidating and emotionally abusive during their arguments, and April almost always backs down.

Core fear and purpose of control. If John sounds a bit like you, then you probably didn't have a significantly high score in any single category. Instead, you scored fairly evenly on the entire questionnaire. This is why the personality type *"There's Nothing Wrong with Me"* does not appear on the scoring key. You may also identify with John because although you don't have a definite personality style as identified in the other types, you do have a rigid masculine identity and traditional beliefs about relationships. As a result, your core fear is being seen as unmasculine or weak. Because you associate weakness and emotional attachments with women, you control in order to maintain your masculinity and to keep your partner available, but not close.

Triggers and tactics. Your primary triggers are the emotional and relationship needs of your partner. It seems she often wants something from you—taking care of a chore or listening to another rambling account of her day. Family life in general is stressful to you. In fact, you find functioning at work comparatively easy because you are frustrated by the demands at home. You probably depend on traditional, outdated male/female roles to control your relationship with your partner. You get angry when she doesn't want to conform to the traditional role you have assigned her. You like marriage, but you struggle with stress and conflict. You become emotionally abusive and intimidating during conflict and when things don't go your way. However, you are not prone to using severe forms of violence because you don't want to injure your partner or face the legal consequences. You are more likely to use verbal abuse and intimidate your partner into seeing things your way by yelling, throwing things, or slamming objects.

Your partner's experience. Your partner initially was attracted to your masculinity. You were strong, sturdy, fearless, and hardworking. She held onto the hope that as the relationship grew, you would become more emotional and intimate. If you are currently in a long-term relationship, it is because your partner sees good in you in spite of your controlling and intimidating behavior. She is disappointed by how emotionally disconnected you are and wants greater spontaneity and passion in your relationship. She is sometimes frustrated that you don't meet her even halfway; she wants you to meet your obligations to her and your family more fully. She is willing to do a lot of the work in maintaining her relationship with you, but she knows she can't do it by herself. She's frustrated because you don't seem to care about her, and she's hurt because what she wants and needs is never very important to you.

What you need to work on. You need to work on challenging your out-of-date beliefs about men and women. You need to become more in touch with your emotions and learn to resolve conflict without using aggression and control. As you become more adept at looking at your own behavior and problems, you are likely to develop the necessary emotional skills to be intimate without control and abuse.

Key points of the "There's Nothing Wrong with Me" personality
- *Core fears:* Being unmanly or weak
- *Purpose of control tactics:* To manage the demands of intimacy and to avoid the stress of emotion in relationships
- *Triggers:* Pressure from his partner for more involvement and intimacy in the relationship; the demands and stresses of family life
- *Preferred tactics:* Emotional abuse, intimidation, occasional physical violence

- *Partner's chief complaint:* "He says he loves me, but he doesn't want to get close to me; I wish he would talk to me about his feelings without blowing up"
- *Self-management tasks:* Emotional awareness, anger management, conflict resolution, and relationship skills

Now What?

What kind of man are you? You may have seen a little of yourself in all six of these personality profiles or feel you fit cleanly in one. We hope the questionnaire has helped you to understand yourself better and to feel more equipped to work on change. The journey of change is demanding, but it is ultimately rewarding for you and those you love. A professional counselor who specializes in domestic abuse will be able to help you with accountability as well as with gaining insight into your core beliefs, personal triggers, and control tactics. A counselor can also help you to develop behavioral strategies to avoid abusive behavior. You will eventually want to work on the underlying emotional issues that support your controlling and abusive beliefs and behaviors, but right now *you need to stop abusing your partner.*

As you become better at acknowledging your controlling and abusive behavior and begin the journey of personal change, your need to control others will be greatly reduced. We control others to get what we want or what we think we need when we are unable to manage ourselves. Now that you are learning what kind of man you are, you can begin the work of managing your thoughts, emotions, and behavior more effectively.

chapter seven

Anything but Feelings

*I*magine a house where you have lived all your life. You have some memories of how the house looked when you were a boy. You may recall your bedroom and its toys and posters and how the living room was decorated for holidays. As an adult you know most of the rooms pretty well, although you're probably most familiar with the living room, the kitchen, and your bedroom. You know what those rooms are like: how the furniture is arranged, what pictures are on the walls. Then there are places you don't go very often—the attic, the basement. There isn't much in the attic. But the basement: you know there's a workshop down there, and there's an old refrigerator, and somewhere in the back where the lightbulb has burned out there's another room with its door shut and padlocked. Although you may not remember it, you put that lock on the door yourself. That room is the place of hearts and guts—your feelings—and you locked the door long ago.

You've spent a lot of time in that house—in the kitchen where you play cards on Saturday nights and in the garage where you have conversations about what to do on the weekend, how to fix this or that, who'll win the Super Bowl. You've lived in the rooms where you use your mind and body, but the room of feelings is buried deep and is mostly forgotten. This is the house you live in.

Feelings play a larger role in your life than you may imagine. Locking them away damages your relationships and deprives you of the richness of life.

Feelings form one of the four basic aspects of being human: we exist as mental, physical, spiritual, and emotional beings. As a man, you use your mental abilities as an integral part of your life. Whether you work on cars or sell insurance, you're thinking about this or that during much of your workday. You are active and aware of your physical self: you build things, you play sports, you have sex. You may have a spiritual life as well; perhaps you are active in a church, or you find peace in nature by fishing or taking walks in the woods.

But if you are like many men, you fail to experience a range of feelings. You miss out on the intimacy of shared sadness at a funeral or the joy at a child's first step. If someone asked you how many distinct feelings there were, you might say ten or fifteen. In fact, a standard list contains around two hundred separate and distinct feelings.

You may not experience a range of emotions, but you probably struggle with an abundance of fear, hurt, and shame. These are the feelings hidden at the very back of that locked basement room. The problem is that you don't allow yourself to experience and process these disturbing feelings. Instead, you often unknowingly attempt to ease the pain of these feelings in ways that are destructive to yourself and your partner. It could be said that many of the problems of our society—addiction, aggression, assault, homicide, suicide, drunk driving, war—are largely the result of men who act out because they can't handle their most painful and hidden feelings. "Anything but feelings" is one of the unspoken principles of our lives.

Why? For the same reason that men exert power and control over others and avoid and devalue anything that looks like "girl" behavior: male socialization. Although male infants actually show a similar or greater range of feelings and need for nurture than females, by the time they are five years old, most boys have taken on the role of the tough guy. We think they're cute when they show their muscles or pretend to be in charge. Their behavior is less amusing when as adults they need to prove that they're impervious to anything, including the "soft" part of themselves. Most men see feelings as something that gets in the way of doing business and getting things done. They make men look weak. They're messy and pointless.

We'd like you to step back and rethink your ideas about feelings. If you do, we believe you'll let yourself experience more feelings, and as a result you'll have a fuller and more satisfying life and a more loving relationship. More important, you'll be much less likely to harm your partner and more likely to give her the intimacy she wants—and needs.

Hurt, Fear, and Shame

Men attend anger management programs because they think their anger leads them to hurt their partners, but as you have learned, what really causes domestic abuse is the need to control. Men control women because they've been socialized to believe that men should be dominant. They also control because they don't effectively manage their feelings—especially the deep-rooted feelings of hurt, fear, and shame. They turn these feelings into anger because anger temporarily dulls the pain and lets them counter the sense of smallness and incompetence that accompanies these emotions.

Whenever someone is angry, you can bet that anger is the tip of the iceberg and that other, more painful feelings lie underneath the surface. In the diagram showing the iceberg of unacknowledged and poorly managed feelings, note that the emotions of hurt, fear, and shame are below the water. The tip of the iceberg—the part we can easily see—shows the symptoms or results of the submerged feelings.

Anger Iceberg: Hurt, Fear, Shame

Fear, hurt, and shame—the core feelings locked in the ice—show themselves in different ways. For example, let's say you come home and your partner's car is packed and she's ready to leave you. You probably wouldn't say to yourself, "Gosh, I'm experiencing a core feeling of fear." More likely, you would be overwhelmed by a confusion of feelings: the fear of abandonment, the hurt of being rejected and unloved, possibly the fear of being unlovable. You may feel powerless (you know she's really leaving this time), and you may feel miserable, revengeful, and misunderstood.

Let's look at another example. Let's say Cindy has been working long hours. She makes more money than Ben does—a lot more—but he believes they'd have enough if she had a less high-powered job or didn't work at all. Why can't she come home at five o'clock like normal people? One day she gets home at seven. Ben grabs her by the shoulders, leans into her face, and tells her that she's going to quit her job or he'll leave her. Anger has displaced Ben's core feeling of shame that he can't dominate Cindy. He doesn't feel important as a man; he makes less money than she does and she won't do what he says. He turns his shame and insecurity into anger and lays out ultimatums that temporarily make him feel better but in the long run have the opposite effect of what he wants. Cindy is frightened when he grabs and shouts at her. She is angry and afraid when he threatens to leave her. If this weren't enough, his demand that she quit her job makes her question whether she wants to be in the relationship at all.

We urge you to study the list below and mark all the feelings you have experienced. This is only a partial list, and some of these feelings may be more familiar to you than others. Watch particularly for the ones that trigger your anger or other acting-out behaviors.

Fear	*Hurt*	*Shame*
afraid	abandoned	ashamed
anxious	despairing	cheated
apprehensive	despondent	defeated
cautious	injured	depressed
cowardly	lonely	disregarded
fearful	miserable	disappointed
helpless	misunderstood	discontented
hesitant	pained	exploited
insecure	regretful	flawed
overwhelmed	rejected	foolish
powerless	resentful	gullible
provoked	revengeful	helpless
reluctant	self-pitying	inferior
suspicious	stunned	invalidated
uncomfortable	unloved	powerless
uneasy	unsure	unlovable
unsafe	unworthy	used
worried	wounded	

Managing Your Feelings

Think about the expressions we hear from other guys: "suck it up" or "tough it out" or "deal with it." In working with men to help them manage their feelings, we tell them to do just about the opposite: "let it out" or "soften up." Here are four key elements to managing your feelings so you avoid the need for control and the anger-fueled impulse to abuse.

Experience. Okay, as you've guessed, we are asking you to undo a lifetime of ignoring, denying, and burying your core feelings. By this point in your life you are probably mostly numb to them. And when you begin to experience an unpleasant feeling, you immediately block it out or transform it into anger. Instead, you need to let these difficult feelings wash over you. They won't kill you. Say to yourself: "God, I feel awful. How could Diane hurt me so much? How does she have such power? I can't even think straight. I guess this relationship was more important than I thought." If you can't manage this little speech to yourself, at least fight the impulse to kick the feelings aside or turn them into anger. Fight with everything you've got. How do you do that?

First, stop and calm yourself. When we get upset—especially when we are angry or scared—we go into attack mode. Our breathing becomes shallow and our hearts beat faster. You don't want to lose yourself in the anger or fear of attack mode. Instead, breathe deeply to slow yourself down—to let yourself experience your feelings but not be overwhelmed by them.

Second, get grounded, literally, by putting your feet on the ground and standing up straight. Loosen up your body by unclenching your neck, shoulders, jaw, fists, forehead, and other places of tension. Try to unwind the knot you feel in your chest or stomach.

Third—and this will take practice—thoughtfully consider your emotional reaction. When you react to core fears without thinking about what you are doing, you remain trapped in old patterns of behavior. Before you know it, your hurt or fear has been channeled into anger and you are ready to lash out or blame someone else. In contrast, when you are aware of your thoughts and feelings and reactions you will not be swamped by them.

Did you watch snapping turtles when you were a kid? They'd snap at a stick because they're hardwired to do that. As human beings, as mature men, we can experience our feelings, think, consider, and reflect while calming ourselves down. We don't have to snap.

Identify. Driving down the road, most men can identify most cars: make, model, and maybe even year. That's literally hundreds of vehicles, often with small differences between them. But most men have difficulty naming even a few feelings, to say nothing at all of identifying feelings they have recently experienced. This is such a common problem that psychologists and psychiatrists have a name for the inability to identify feelings: *alexithymia.*

There are many reasons why you might not experience and identify particular feelings, but anger is a chief reason. Anger is the bully of feelings. If you are riddled with rage or just pretty darned angry, the feelings you need to find have been pushed aside. Your job is to find them and name them.

Anger plays out on a continuum, a band of increasing tension. At one end are minor irritations, such as traffic that makes your drive to work a little longer. Somewhere in the middle, clearly angry, a serious argument with your partner, or being accused at work of something you didn't do. At the far end lies rage. Rage is when you see red. Rage makes perceiving reality difficult because it highjacks your thinking self. You end up not being able to put situations and people in perspective. Little things become big. The inferno of rage doesn't let you see the fireflies in your life.

Ask yourself these questions to help free your other feelings from being bullied by anger.

- Am I blaming others for my anger, focusing on them and therefore not looking at myself and my real feelings?
- What's happening inside of me—my thoughts and feelings—that is triggering my rage? What is the real feeling? (Look back at the list of feelings: which seems to fit best?)
- What old wounds are being triggered in me? Most of the time, my partner (or other person) is not the real source of my rage; she (or he) is only a catalyst.
- Do I really want to engage in destructive behavior such as yelling, hitting, drinking, or drugging?

Suppose that Elias's boss has threatened to fire him. If Elias reacts without identifying his underlying feelings, he will avoid the pain and confusion of those feelings by turning them into anger. But if he takes some deep breaths, stands up straight, and relaxes his body, he will be able to look at the situation to find his real feelings. If he can stop and reflect, he'll realize he feels stunned, betrayed, and afraid. When he takes the time, he realizes that his fear is unwarranted: he knows that his boss's threat is empty—merely an act of frustration—because his boss's manager wouldn't allow Elias to be fired. Elias is a valued employee. If he gives himself enough time, Elias can remember that his boss can be a pretty emotional guy, that he's been under a lot of pressure, and that he was probably letting off steam. Elias might even be able to have some sympathy for him. By identifying his fears instead of instantly turning them into anger, Elias will be able to defend himself and his job calmly and rationally.

Think. Remember that your thinking creates and reinforces your feelings. Imagine that your partner has told you that she doesn't think there's enough money to buy the plasma TV you really want. Your immediate response is to think: "This is crap. I don't deserve to be treated this way. I never get anything I want around here. She's a jerk and she's always been a jerk. It's unfair. I hate it. I'll give her a piece of my mind." This internal response to your partner is an example of *self-talk*. We constantly have conversations in our heads, either with ourselves or other people. Self-talk is powerful because it helps to direct your behavior. If your self-talk is angry and concentrates on how you have been wronged, it will fuel bad feelings and you will continue to get worked up and angry. In this case, your angry response is created because you haven't stopped long enough to identify your feelings. How *do* you feel when your partner says you can't afford a plasma television? Before you get angry, you may feel *rejected* (she doesn't want me to be happy), *anxious* (I'm not in control of the situation), and *disrespected* (she should agree with me because I'm the man). You can sweep away these uncomfortable feelings by getting angry instead of experiencing and identifying them.

You can, on the other hand, say to yourself: "I don't want to think this way or feel this anger. I'm going to think of another way to respond." What else might you say? Well, you could ask her why she thinks you can't afford the new TV. Or you could drop the discussion for now—*do not argue with her*—and think about the issue quietly and calmly. "Maybe she's right," you could say to yourself. "She isn't trying to make me feel bad—maybe she's worried we won't have money for something else." After you've experienced and identified your feelings, think about them. Watch them, and then let them go. Say to yourself: "This is not a big deal. Everything's going to be okay. Things have a way of working out." With practice, you will experience the satisfaction of watching your angry feelings recede so that you can more calmly manage your true feelings.

Express. Most men are nervous about expressing their feelings. It's hard to talk about something you don't experience and can't name. Imagine trying to tell someone what it's like to swim in the ocean when you can't remember the experience and you don't know the words to describe it. Men know they're in an arena where they haven't played much when they try to talk about feelings; they feel inadequate, and men don't like to feel inadequate. If they're trapped in situations in which talking about their feelings is required, they hem and haw, embarrassed because they know they ought to be able to do such a natural thing.

Like any activity, expressing what you're feeling takes time and effort to learn. If you haven't talked much about your feelings, start with small steps. Commit yourself to telling your partner one thing every day that you have felt or noticed. Try complimenting her, or saying something like "I'm worried about Joey—he seems to be spending so much time alone lately" or "I feel very close to you right now" (but only if you do). Eventually, with practice, you can tell her that you are anxious or disappointed or scared rather than acting out. And you know what's even better? You can learn to tell her that you are happy, or that you love her, or that you are grateful that she does such a good job taking care of you and the kids, *because you will genuinely feel those emotions.*

Loving Our Feelings

Feelings make us more alive. If you put your mind to it, you can probably make a list of ten or twelve times that you've been very much aware of your feelings. Perhaps it was shock at the death of someone you love. Or relief that you didn't lose your driver's license. The joy of catching a really big walleye. Your nervousness before a job interview. The gratitude when your wife or girlfriend said "Yes." The warmth of your mom's hug. These were times when you felt particularly alive. Your pulse quickened and you felt a flood of feeling rush over you.

Scientists are slowly identifying the chemicals in our brains, such as serotonin and dopamine, that affect our feelings. And while there's a lot to be learned from the research, the significant fact is that experiencing a full range of feelings enriches our lives. When we don't experience or express feelings, we are only partly alive.

Feelings help us connect with our partners. Relationships are about many things: sharing a home, raising children, taking vacations together, taking care of one another. But people can do those things without having an intimate relationship, and it's intimacy that creates true relationship between a man and a woman. Many people have their own notion of what *intimacy* means. Intimacy is a bond, a feeling of closeness, a sense that you know a person very well, the repeated discovery that you share things that are almost inexpressible. Even though you may try to stay away from your feelings, the place you can't afford to ignore them is in relationships. Intimacy is about feelings. Many people, especially men, believe that sex is intimacy. When we use the word *intimacy* in our groups, participants sometimes smirk, thinking that we're talking about sex. During an intake assessment with Dean, a forty-four-year-old machinist, Randy asked about the level of intimacy in Dean's relationship with his partner, Linda. Dean looked down, then up, while tapping his fingers on his knee. Randy waited patiently, knowing he had asked a complex question. Dean eventually answered, "Oh, we have sex about a couple of times a week on average." For Dean, intimacy was sex. There should be intimacy in sex.

But most of us know the difference between sleeping with a woman we hardly know and one we feel close to. After we make love to a woman we love, it feels like a waste to have sex with someone else. That's the intimacy difference.

Some of the work we've suggested here you can start by yourself. Other pieces, particularly getting the lock open on that basement room, may require extra help. A qualified therapist can help you find the padlock key you are looking for.

Not being in touch with your feelings is like driving a car without gauges. You don't know what's going on under the hood. You don't know how fast you're going or how much gas is left in the tank or if the engine is overheating. You can make some guesses by using your observation and past experience, but sometimes guesses turn out to be wrong. You can be driving 110 miles per hour and not know it. Experience, identify, think about, and express your feelings. You'll find yourself cruising—not too fast, not too slow. Just about right to get where you're going.

chapter eight

Missing Links
Empathy and Accountability

Randy's friend, Beth. Several years ago, my dear college friend Beth was raped by a man who broke into her house and waited for her to get home. He tackled her in the kitchen, dragged her to her bedroom, tied her to her bed, and blindfolded her. He raped and abused her for over two hours.

Earlier that evening, Beth had enjoyed dinner with old college friends, laughing and teasing about good times. Afterward, she looked forward to going home. It was the first house she'd ever owned, and she loved it. She tended the small garden, puttered about in the basement work-shop, and shared cookies with the neighborhood children. She felt safe there.

The day after the rape, the men and women in Beth's life moved her out of her home because they knew she could never feel safe there again.

Several weeks later, we talked about that night. I asked Beth, "How could someone do that to you? How are individuals capable of such horrible acts?"

Her eyes filled with tears as she took a sip of coffee. She looked at me and said, "Randy, if he knew what he was doing to me, to my soul, he wouldn't have been able to do it."

For me, that was a moment of great clarity. Beth helped me to understand what can help abusive men to stop hurting others. The enemy of abuse is empathy. *Empathy is an emotional connection to another person's experience.* It's the pain you feel when your seven-year-old daughter comes home crying after being teased by older neighborhood girls. Your heart goes out to her because you love her and because you remember what it's like to be teased or bullied by older kids. Empathy helps you understand and sympathize with the anger, sadness, and fear that may face an older relative when he learns he has only six months to live. Empathy increases your happiness when you can sincerely share and feel another's joy.

Because empathy propels you to understand and care for others, it keeps you from hurting them. People who have inadequate empathy not only don't care when they see other people in pain, they also don't care if they cause pain to others. What you may have done to your partner probably isn't as extreme as what the rapist did to Beth. The likelihood is, however, that you allowed yourself to abuse your partner because you weren't fully aware of her as a person with feelings, needs, and wants. This is what Beth meant when she told Randy that if her attacker had known "what he was doing to me, to my soul, he wouldn't have been able to do it."

A poverty of empathy is a source of abuse and violence.

Stunted Empathy

The process of male socialization explains many of the causes of stunted empathy. *Stunted* isn't meant as an insulting term— here, it means that the growth and development of your empathy was hindered or stopped completely. You were taught to block yourself from feeling empathy for another boy's physical pain by coaches who screamed "Hit him, hurt him!"

If you told some other boy that you felt sorry for someone, you were accused of being a sissy. You probably didn't know the actual word *empathy* in middle school, but you certainly knew that it was only for girls. Tough guys aren't bothered by feelings, right? But as a boy being socialized into manhood, you were sometimes hurt, scared, and shamed, and those painful feelings did bother you. To lessen the pain, you channeled those feelings into a numbing anger that may continue to stunt your sense of empathy. So you can call your partner names, yell at her at the top of your lungs, push her or grab her, and not see the pain and fear you are causing. Your moral compass no longer points north, and you turn into an abusive man.

This is what happened to Tom (chapter 5, "The Dynamics of Domestic Abuse"). Tom wasn't blind to the immediate consequences of his abusive behavior. He knew the instant he hit Sally that he had broken a bond of trust between them. What he didn't know was that the bond was cracked long before that night and that it was his own controlling, oppressive behavior that drove Sally away from him.

Sally's story. "It was after the boys were born that I began to get nervous around Tom. At first I ignored him because I thought he was just nagging when he said I should cook more and not be out in the evenings and not spend so much time at my parents' house. But he wasn't just nagging—he was serious. He insisted that I had to be home every evening when he got home from work and have dinner ready, too. I hate cooking, and besides, he always got home at different times. He wanted me to give up my job at the museum after Aaron was born. I think he wanted to change me into a perfect little housewife and keep me all to himself. He never liked my friends or family. When my girlfriends were at the house he'd act like they weren't there, and he was always cool with my parents. He acted as though loving friends and family was the same as cheating on him.

"It got so I really *was* spending more time with my mom because he was always so critical at home. I tried to change to please him, but it was never enough. When I tried to talk to him he'd clam up, and by last year we weren't talking much at all, except for his lectures to me about how I should do things and why no one else would want me. There wasn't much going on in the bedroom, either. I don't know why he thought insulting me would make me want to have sex with him. But I never really considered leaving him until he hit me. I was terrified before that—when he threw the beer bottle—because I didn't know what he'd do next, and I knew I wouldn't be able to defend myself and protect Aaron and Jason. Why did he have to do that? Why did he have to wreck our family by doing that? He's been doing a lot better since he started counseling, and I really don't want a divorce. But it will take a long time to really trust him again."

Causes and Consequences

Tom's actions. Tom wanted Sally to behave like *his* idea of a good wife. So he lectured her about spending too much money and how to improve her spending habits, how to cook dinner, when she should be home, and how she should pay more attention to him and less to her family and friends. He wanted her available to him whenever he felt like it. He pressured her to have children and quit her job before she was ready. He was rude to her friends and barely civil to her parents. He told her that since she wasn't very attractive no one else would want her, so she had better do as he told her. In other words, Tom used the tactics of threats, isolation, economic abuse, male privilege, and emotional abuse to try to gain control over Sally and to force her to be the woman he wanted.

Consequences of Tom's actions. But if you listen closely, you can hear in Sally's story the undesirable consequences of Tom's attempts to control her. At first, Sally did try to go along with Tom. She had children before she was ready and she quit the job she loved. She saw less of her friends and tried to visit her mother when Tom was at work. She even attempted cooking, although she knew Tom would criticize whatever she put on the table.

But in spite of her efforts, Tom's abusive attempts at control increased rather than decreased because he was still responding to his unexamined assumptions about men and women and his fears of abandonment. Sally realized that she could never do enough to please him, and she began to pull away from Tom in self-defense. His constant criticisms made her anxious and unhappy in her own home. As a result, she managed to be gone more in the evenings, even with two young children. She spent more time with her mother, who, unlike Tom, supported Sally and loved her unconditionally. Sally had less and less interest in sex with Tom. She spent more money, rather than less, to try to establish a little independence from him. She gave up on dinner. Tom complained that there wasn't any food in the fridge on the night he hit her, and he was right. Although Sally made sure Aaron and Jason ate well, she didn't go out of her way to shop for Tom.

In other words, *the more Tom controlled, the more Sally pulled away.* Tom saw her responses as further evidence that she was a poor wife, so he increased his efforts to control her. These increased attempts at control didn't "improve" Sally. Instead, she suffered the predictable results of Tom's abuse tactics. Her self-esteem decreased; she lost interest in sex;

she spent more money; she tried to be away as much as possible; she grew anxious and afraid around Tom; and she didn't want to try to love and care for him. Tom had trapped them in the cycle of abuse that is pictured below.

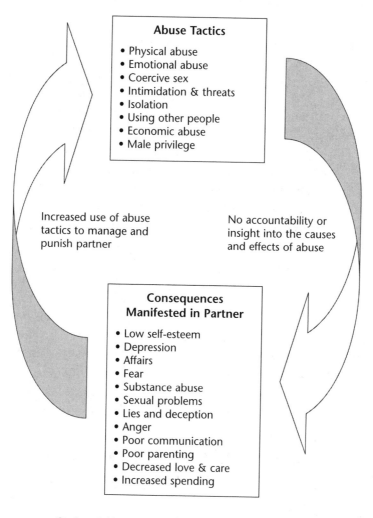

Cycle of Abusive Behavior and Consequences

Randy's client, Larry. Larry was a second-generation interstate trucker whose work frequently kept him away from home for days. He felt disconnected from his wife, and worse, when he came home it sometimes seemed that she didn't even want to be with him.

Larry was convicted of domestic abuse and referred to my group after throwing his wife, Clara, to the ground in front of their house. After he'd completed the group, he continued attending individual sessions. Larry brought Clara and their three-year-old son, Christopher, to one of his scheduled individual appointments. I asked Clara privately if she wanted to be a part of the session, and she said yes. At one point, Larry didn't like something that Clara said, and he began yelling at her. Clearly pained and afraid, she turned her face from him, stood up, and walked across my office to help Christopher play on the floor. Larry said to me in disgust, "See, Randy, she ignores me like that all the time. That's why I get so angry." He clearly thought that I would agree with him and tell Clara to rejoin us.

Larry was like a poster boy for the Cycle of Abusive Behavior and Consequences. I've never seen a couple enact the steps so quickly. Of course, they had had plenty of practice; Larry had been abusive from the first year of their marriage. It was obvious to me and to Clara why she turned away from him, but Larry did not understand that his abusive behavior was guaranteed to make Clara want to get away. In fact, Clara lost hope that he would ever change, especially after a year of counseling. She eventually left Larry.

Stopping the Cycle: Empathy and Accountability

What can Tom or Larry—or, more important, you—do to stop this painful, unproductive cycle? There are two main things to work on: empathy and accountability. We have separated these qualities to discuss them, but in fact they go hand in hand.

Empathy. Your sense of empathy may have been stunted, but that doesn't mean you can't increase it. Fortunately, empathy isn't like a plant or a puppy. If young, growing things are deprived of care and nutrients, they may never achieve their full size and strength. But empathy is not a spindly tree or the runt of the litter. It is a skill, not a gift of nature, and that means that you can practice and improve.

You can learn to identify and manage the fears that undermine your empathy for your partner. You can put yourself in her shoes and try to imagine life with a partner who constantly humiliated you, belittled you, threatened your physical safety, and kept you from achieving happiness in your life. To achieve empathy for your partner, you must be accountable for your actions.

Accountability. Tom knew that he broke more than the beer bottle that night, although he didn't want to admit it to himself and he tried to minimize his behavior to the police. At his first group meeting, he announced that Sally should be in a group to learn how to be a good wife. Other men use other cover-up tactics to spotlight their partner's failings rather than their own. Men in our groups will say, "I don't have an abuse problem; she's a poor communicator" or "I don't have a control problem; she just spends too much" or "I don't have an anger problem; she just doesn't listen to me."

Despite your efforts to disconnect yourself from your abusive behavior, using power and control tactics to get what you want leads to undesirable consequences, just as using alcohol does. The alcoholic in denial may tell us woeful stories of loss, conflict, and setbacks, but without making the connection between his out-of-control life and his abusive drinking. Stopping the drinking and understanding the effect it has on his life is the first step in his recovery, just as it is with abuse and control. The cycle will not stop and you and your partner will never have a loving relationship if you do not accept responsibility for your actions and their consequences. Poor accountability perpetuates the cycle.

How do empathy and accountability work together?

If you refuse to accept accountability for your behavior, you will never be able to genuinely feel the effects of your abuse on your partner. If you cannot feel the pain, fear, and heartbreak your abuse causes her, you will never feel the need to be accountable for your behavior. Empathy and accountability are like links in a chain. If even one is weak or broken, the chain will fall apart.

As you increase your sense of empathy and accountability, you will be able to make the right choices. You will discover more personal power and peace as you focus on your own growth and let your partner be who she is. The more you let go, the more you will create what you desire—a loving relationship with your partner.

Remember that abusive behavior creates an accumulation of consequences in your partner. Stopping the abuse today doesn't stop her pain, anger, and distrust of you today. She can only begin to heal once she feels safe, respected, and honored. When you can provide her this sacred space, then you are contributing to her healing process. That's all you can do; you can't control her healing process. You can't force it to happen. You can't speed it up. The healing process may take years. You have to let go of her with respect and love. To do anything less is to enter back into the cycle. And, let's face it, to use the same controlling tactics and expect different results would be insanity. Love, trust, and intimacy are cultivated by acting in loving, trustworthy, and empathic ways.

chapter nine

Sons and Daughters

I magine yourself sitting in your living room looking out at
your front yard. Across the street, an angry, shouting man
is hitting your six-year-old son. In an instant the hair rises
on your neck, adrenaline surges through your body, your
muscles tighten, and you leap up so fast you knock over the
coffee table. As you dart out the front door, you begin shouting. You race across the street without even checking for
traffic. You feel compelled to protect your son at any cost.
You will do what it takes to get across that road and stop the
abuse. You love your child, you see the danger, and you respond without a second thought.

> **You are the man across the street.**

Before you jump out of your chair to protest that you're
a good dad and have never abused your children, let's look
a little deeper.

"I Would _Never_ Hurt My Kids!"

When Randy first asked John what sort of father he was,
John replied without hesitation, "I'm a good dad. I try to

get to Billy's soccer games on the weekends, I help him with his homework, and I make sure Emily and I don't argue in front of him. Kids shouldn't have to listen to their parents' fighting."

John's idea of arguing with Emily was starting a fight and slamming her into the refrigerator when she didn't go along with him. In his eyes, his statement was true: he was very careful not to let Billy, their son, witness him physically or verbally abuse Emily. When Randy raised his eyebrows, John responded emphatically, "I would *never* hurt my kids!"

The truth is that any man who abuses his partner also abuses the children. It's easy to agree that directly abusing children will negatively affect them, and most men will agree that children who see their mother physically abused will also be negatively affected. But abuse contaminates children's lives in other, less obvious ways. This is because the *relationships* among members of a family inevitably affect every other member. (By *family*, we mean any group of adults and children living together. If you are a sometimes sleepover boyfriend, you're included in this definition, too.) Teenage siblings who fight constantly can cause a headache for their entire family, for example, and a parent who plays favorites can cause deep rifts among the children involved. In the same way, your physical or emotional abuse of your partner will inevitably reach your children. Even if, like John, you don't let your children see or hear you abuse their mother, they will still be injured because of their close relationship with her. The greatest source of trauma for children is damage to their relationship with their mothers.

Abusive men damage their children's emotional health and development in four basic ways:

- by abusing the children's mother in front of them
- by using the children as a tool to control and abuse their partners

- by affecting the relationship between the children and their mother
- by directly mistreating, abusing, or neglecting the children

The first form of abuse:
When children directly witness domestic abuse

Surprisingly, children who witness domestic abuse of their mothers are more damaged than children who are physically abused themselves. Children suffer when they see or hear domestic abuse. They have problems with sleep, acting out, poor grades, sadness, anxiety, and lowered self-esteem. The legacy of domestic abuse will likely follow them into their adult lives. Children who witness domestic abuse are far more likely to be in abusive relationships as adults than are children who do not come from abusive homes. In other words, your daughter is likely to marry an abusive man. She has learned that there isn't much you can do about abuse, so you might as well put up with it. Your son will learn that abuse and control are effective in getting his own way, and knowing little else, he will be more likely to be abusive and controlling in his intimate relationships. This is an ugly legacy that will continue into the next generation, until someone stands up with accountability and courage and begins the journey of change.

John's son, Billy, was nine years old when he started seeing Randy. His parents were concerned about his drop in grades and his bullying of other boys in the neighborhood and at school. Billy was nervous, constantly looking around the office, quick to be startled when Randy moved or when sounds penetrated the office walls from outside. Billy talked about how mad he got at other kids (because they were "stupid") and how he was frequently in trouble at school for fighting. As Billy fidgeted in his seat, Randy asked, "Do you ever get mad at home?"

Billy looked down with sudden interest at his untied sneaker and, while tying it, muttered to the floor, "Well, I get mad when my dad yells and pushes Mom. He thinks I don't know, but I do."

Randy leaned forward in his chair to make eye contact with Billy when he lifted his head from his shoe. "Do you get scared, too?"

"I'm not scared, just mad. I want to hit my Dad and make him stop."

Randy probed, "But don't you get scared that your mom is going to get hurt?"

Billy put his head down to hide his emerging tears. "When Mom starts crying, I get scared," he eventually responded. "I don't know why he hurts her like that."

Billy is growing up in a household where he is learning to bury his rage and fear. He has learned to protect himself by scaring others first. He has learned that being small and vulnerable around others who are more powerful is danger-ous: it is better to take control and be the powerful, intimi-dating one. At nine these emotions and unspoken thoughts spill out on the playground, resulting in fistfights at school. At twenty-nine he may find himself abusing his own wife.

The second form of abuse:
When a man uses the children as a tool to control his partner

Let's say John wants to make Emily stay home with him rather than leave on her once-a-month girls' night out. Instead of stating this need directly, he tries to make her feel guilty by saying she's neglecting Billy. A good mother, he points out, would stay home and help Billy finish the science project that they've both been working on. John may believe that he is genuinely advocating for his son, and perhaps this may be true at times, but the main driving force behind his false claim is the desire to control Emily.

A man may also use his children as go-betweens by telling them information that will make them more loyal and attached to him, while eroding their love and attachment to their mother. This particularly happens in relationships in which separation and divorce are likely. A controlling man can set up his partner to choose between her children and the marriage. In other words, he brings her back into the relationship by making it apparent to her that she will lose her children along with her marriage if she divorces.

Once Emily began to learn that Billy's home life was related to his poor behavior, she began making plans for divorce. Although Emily filed for a personal protection order (PPO) against John on her own behalf, she was certain that John would not harm Billy, and he was allowed to see Billy without supervision. John's distorted thinking had allowed him to believe for years that he was a good father and that he and Emily suffered the normal arguments of married life. He found himself quite distraught when his family began breaking up. He began telling Billy that the break-up was his mother's fault and that the PPO was filed as an attempt to keep him away from Billy. He didn't, however, admit how the years of abuse had caused Emily to fear him and worry for their son. Although Billy knew about some of the abuse, he had never experienced it himself, and he wasn't ready to give up his father completely. John persuaded him that the divorce was Emily's idea and that it would mean father and son wouldn't be able to see each other. Over time, Billy became angry with his mother, and he began acting out with her as well as at school. Emily found it increasingly difficult to provide adequate parenting for Billy while managing the separation. She eventually stopped divorce proceedings and moved back in with John because he threatened a custody suit, and she feared losing her son more than she feared her husband. John's argument for gaining custody of Billy was convincing: his mother clearly couldn't handle him, but Billy was fine when he was in his father's care. Emily returned out of fear, not love.

John's actions show how effective using children can be in controlling our partners, but they also demonstrate how remarkably damaging such actions can be to the relationships among all the family members. Kids can conclude that their mother and her problems caused the dissolution of the family rather than learning that their father's violence, abuse, and control have negative, life-changing consequences for themselves and their mother.

The third form of abuse:
 When a man abuses his partner and thus damages the mother-child relationship

Abuse takes its toll on your partner. She is likely to get depressed, nervous, and anxious about her ability to do anything right. This downward spiral of emotions can lead to poor parenting on her part, either by being emotionally unavailable to the kids or by being too emotional with them. Moreover, people who are abused and controlled are angry, but they can't express their rage directly to their abuser. As a result, they are at risk of acting out their angry feelings on others less powerful than they are. Where else does the buck stop except with the most vulnerable members of the family? This result is directly abusive to children. No amount of "good dad" behavior can make up for it.

Charlie relates that Pam came in for a collateral session to help describe her partner Stan's abusive behavior. She managed a little opening small talk with Charlie but then began to cry and concentrated on staring at the floor. Charlie assured her, "Pam, it's okay to cry. Please tell me what's going on."

Pam related how bad she felt about her treatment of her

two daughters. "I get so angry with them sometimes over nothing, and other times, when they really are acting up, I don't do anything about it. They never know what to expect from me." She was silent. "Sometimes I just feel like crawling into a hole."

Stan's chronic abuse had left Pam depressed and exhausted. She was always tired and often fearful of his behavior. Knowing that she needed her energy to deal with Stan in the evenings, she guiltily shortchanged their daughters. Sometimes, she explained, she would turn on the TV rather than play with them or take them to the park because if the house and dinner weren't just right when he arrived home, he would become angry and verbally abusive.

Charlie recalled that while Stan admitted abusing Pam, he was adamant that the girls weren't affected because he rarely yelled in front of them. In fact, Stan worried about his daughters because he believed that Pam didn't spend enough time with them and was not an effective disciplinarian. Charlie knew it was crucial for Stan to make the connection between his treatment of Pam and her poor parenting, because if Stan understood the impact his behavior had on Pam *and the girls,* it could be part of the motivation he needed to stop hurting Pam.

The final form of abuse:
When a man directly mistreats, abuses, or neglects his children

Men who practice controlling and abusive behavior in their intimate relationships with their partners often perpetrate such behavior as fathers. Most parents know that children require sacrifices of time, effort, money, and energy. An abusive father, in contrast, knows that controlling behavior will protect him from meeting the needs of his children. Because he believes his needs are the most important in the family, he doesn't feel guilty about neglecting or abusing his children to get what he wants. He may not even be aware that he consistently puts his own desires before the needs of his kids. The man who plays video games all evening after work doesn't see himself as a neglectful father ("I just spent all day at work!"), but in terms of the time he spends with his children, he might as well stay at work.

Just as power and control tactics can get an abusive man's partner to behave as he wishes, such behavior can force his children to do what he wants. Children will obey out of fear, but their obedience should never be mistaken for love or respect. As children grow older, an abusive father is likely to be confronted by his children's attempts to challenge his authoritative control.

Marie, the sixteen-year-old stepdaughter of Charlie's client Eric, got into trouble as a minor in possession of drugs. The terms of Marie's probation required her to see a counselor. At first, Eric told Charlie, Marie made it clear to anyone who would listen that counseling was "a stupid waste of time." But over time, Marie began warming up to the idea of expressing her feelings about her stepfather in a safe environment. Eventually, she felt strong enough to tell him what she thought of him. Eric related that her hatred and contempt caught him off guard. "But kids need discipline, especially teenagers," he told Charlie. "She'll get over it."

Eric's idea of "discipline" for his stepdaughter was the same controlling and verbally abusive behavior he used against his wife, Tracy. Eric deflected attention from his own shortcomings and tried to build himself up by constantly pointing out that nothing Tracy and Marie did was ever good enough; there was always room for improvement. Even as a little girl Marie was subjected to criticism that stunted her self-esteem. She desperately wanted Eric's approval, love, and acceptance, but instead found only rejection, anger, and contempt. As a teenager she turned to alcohol both for relief and to act out against her stepfather. She tried to quiet her self-doubt and sense of powerlessness by finding a group of friends who encouraged drinking and taking risks.

Through working with Charlie, Eric slowly learned to subdue his abusive criticisms of Tracy and Marie, but he clung to the idea that he was a good father. He blamed Tracy for Marie's drinking, saying that she was "too soft" on her daughter. Like so many of the abusive fathers we see, Eric was in denial about the negative effects his abusive actions had on his family.

Stop the Denial and Stop the Pain

You may have a Marie or a Billy in your house. It is crucial for you to understand and take responsibility for the devastating effects your abusive and controlling behavior can have on the children in your life. *Only you are in a position either to pass the pain of your own life onto your children or to stop the generational cycle of abuse.* We hope that knowing this can help motivate you to take on the difficult work of changing. Children cannot thrive if they are denied an emotionally and physically safe environment. Because one of the most abusive and damaging things a father can do to his children is to abuse their mother, the children in your family need you to be not only a good father but also a loving husband.

Just remember how you would respond if you saw your young son being hurt and frightened by a stranger outside your house. The stranger is you, the father your son wants so badly to love and trust. He needs to see you treat his mother with respect and love, not abuse and control.

chapter ten

Loving Relationships

So far we have offered ideas about the background of your need to control. We've looked at lies you tell yourself and lies you may have been told as you were growing up, lies intended to "turn you into a man." You've seen how the cycle of domestic abuse works, and you've had a chance to consider your personality type. We've given you suggestions about what triggers your controlling and abusive behavior and how to avoid it. We hope you've given yourself time to think about all these ideas. If you're in a relationship, we hope you accept that your first obligation is to let go of your abusive and controlling behavior. That will make your relationship more respectful and stable. But it's not enough just to avoid abusive behavior; you need to initiate positive behaviors as well. Holding yourself back from abuse is good, but you have to reach out to your partner as well.

Charlie Remembers . . .

A long time ago, when I was in my early twenties and lived as a hungry grad student in an apartment in downtown Detroit, I had a neighbor named Ellen. She had just ended a painful divorce, and sitting at my kitchen table one cold January afternoon, she sadly told me about the demise of their relationship. I remember that she said: "Harold and I had a pretty good relationship. But we wanted it to get better, so we got married. It turned out that things didn't really change very much. We were so much in love. But we were both just so disappointed in marriage."

That was long before I became a therapist, but even then I was shocked by their misconception about marriage. Ellen and Harold apparently lived under the disastrous belief that marriage will make something good happen to you. They believed that simply by being married they would naturally become closer and develop an intimate, loving life together. This is a myth, and it's a dangerous myth: if partners don't actively and deliberately love one another, their relationship grows stagnant and potentially becomes a breeding ground for domestic abuse. At best, like Ellen and Harold, couples get divorced because there ceases to be anything to hold them together. At worst, controlling men act out because they don't get what they want, and they act out by hurting the women they mean to love.

What Does a Healthy, Loving Relationship Look Like?

If you want love, intimacy, and affection from your partner, then love her. This means making an effort to love her when you're tired and when she doesn't seem to be loving you back. Loving her means being attentive; it means reaching out and being affectionate or giving even when you don't feel like it. In loving her, you won't think it's the end of the world if you let go of your interests in favor of hers, and it won't be too much effort to do the little things that make your partner feel special. Loving her means nurturing her, supporting her in her interests and work, doing your half and sometimes more of the things that make your household work. It also means observing and monitoring yourself and honestly evaluating your behavior. When you realize you're ignoring your partner or taking her for granted, stop that behavior right away by becoming an engaged and loving partner. Make it your job to be accountable not only for ending hurt but for conceiving love. Stretch yourself. Extend yourself. You'll go places in your growth and with your partner that you never knew existed.

Okay, okay, you're probably saying. Enough of the theory. How does all this actually work? What does it look like? Let's see how a few men from chapter 6 ("What Kind of Man Am I?") would act in a healthy, loving relationship with their partners: Bill ("Don't leave me") and Amanda, Stan ("Leave me alone") and Marilyn, and Gordie ("It's got to be me") and Patricia.

Bill's insecurities run deep. He clings to Amanda in unhealthy ways because he's terrified of being abandoned. How does he respond when Amanda's sister invites her to visit France? He hates the idea, of course. But Bill is committed to working on a healthy relationship. The old Bill would have raged that Amanda was self-centered and never thought of anyone but herself. He would have blown up at the very mention of France, and if Amanda persisted in making plans, he may have become violent. Now, he works on reminding himself of all the ways Amanda shows her love; he tells himself that the ten-day vacation won't last forever; he supports her because he knows she's wanted to take this trip for years. It might not be easy for Bill, but he does the right and loving thing by sending Amanda off to have a good time. Is he miserable while she's gone? Possibly. But because he loved her enough to let her go, Amanda is almost sure to come back.

Stan is a different story. In a loving relationship with Marilyn, Stan does not retreat to the garage every evening to work on his dune buggies. He doesn't give up this hobby, but he doesn't hide behind it to avoid the demands and intimacies of marriage and family life. He makes the effort to be with Marilyn and their children most evenings, even when he would rather be working in the garage. Because he is committed to a loving relationship with Marilyn, he does not blame her for depriving him of his peace and solitude. Instead, he is grateful that she wants to be with him. He helps with homework; he gets the younger kids to bed; he makes time for his wife in which he is fully present, not fantasizing about working alone in the garage.

And Gordie? Gordie loves to love himself, so loving Patricia will be a challenge. If he wants to change, he will need to give up his idea that love is a one-way street. Loving Patricia means focusing on her and giving up his constant demands for her validation and attention. When Patricia wins an award at work, Gordie is the first to celebrate her success. He reminds himself that Patricia deserves to be the center of attention, and he gladly keeps her in the spotlight. For Gordie to have a healthy and loving relationship, he will need to see Patricia's needs as being at least as important as his own, and sometimes more important.

Unlike Charlie's friend Ellen and her former husband, the men from chapter 6 learn that a loving, healthy relationship takes effort. A relationship is like a garden. Without pruning, watering, and fertilizing, it will turn into a bramble of thorns and thistles that will choke out the lovely garden of flowers and vegetables you want to grow. If you do the work, you can have love, the deep and honest and abiding love that you and your partner want. If you don't cultivate your garden, that is, if you don't do the work, you might as well plow it under.

Putting Love in Your Relationship

Like the rest of this book, the suggestions that follow center on you and what you can do, not what you think your partner should do. If you use these suggestions because you think you will be able to control your partner by using loving tactics instead of abusive tactics, then you have missed the entire point. If you cannot give up your need to control, you will never achieve a loving and intimate relationship. But if you are serious about giving up that need, then you are ready to work on creating a relationship of sustained joy, something that you have probably never experienced before. These suggestions will help you take the next steps.

Get your mental health in order

When men enter domestic abuse treatment groups, they often want to go to couples' counseling instead. They insist their problems are caused by their partners or the relationship itself. Not them. They are never the problem, or so they would have you believe. They don't want to work on themselves. She's the one that needs the work! We've already pointed out that you can't change her, and the relationship isn't going to change by itself. So if you want things to get better, that leaves *you*.

So where do you start? First, stop the abuse. Next, get your mental health in order. You are probably thinking, "My mental health is just fine, thank you." But if you have used abuse tactics to control your partner, then you have mental health issues you need to work on. Poor mental health will not allow you to do the work of improving your relationship. Following are some examples of the effects of poor mental health:

- If you are moody or frustrated or depressed, if you use alcohol or drugs too much, if you are distrustful and paranoid, your relationship will not work.
- You may think you get along with everybody, but if you look a little deeper, you may discover that you

are mad at your boss, resentful of siblings, or infuriated with your partner. Remember the iceberg
diagram (chapter 7, "Anything but Feelings")? If
you have been using above-the-waterline anger to
hide the hurt, shame, and fear locked in the ice,
then your mental health needs to improve.

- You may have symptoms of trauma, such as
  high levels of stress, a sense of distrust and wari-
  ness, overreactive anger, deep feelings of insecurity,
  and difficulty expressing feelings or experiencing
  intimacy as a result of being bullied, abused, or
  shamed in childhood.

When these problems are combined with the need to control a partner, creating a loving relationship is difficult.

We'd also like you to think about your day-to-day life. Here
are some questions for you to consider:

- Are you generally happy, upbeat, and full of
  energy? Or do you feel depressed and tired most
  of the time? How much of the time are you angry?
  Are you intense and nervous? Do you have trouble
  relaxing? Do you obsess about perceived wrongs
  that you can't get out of your mind? Do you have
  the attitude that "life sucks and then you die"?
- How do you relate to others? Are you friendly,
  complimentary, and supportive? Or do you keep
  yourself distant by sulking off to your cave in the
  basement or garage? Do you have frequent disagreements? When you disagree with others, do you
  criticize, threaten, and belittle them?
- Can you manage your behavior? When you
  get upset and realize you're going to say or do
  something inappropriate, can you catch yourself

before you do harm? Do you keep yourself from physically hurting others?

- Do you do things in moderation? Or do you practice an excess or overindulgence that causes problems for yourself and others? Do you drink or drug too much? Work too much? Want sex too much? Lose money gambling? Do you need to get an adrenaline rush from extreme sports, driving fast, or buying expensive gadgets?

We're not offering any cutoffs here for what qualifies as mental health or mental illness. This book is not about diagnosing or solving mental health problems. We offer these questions with the hope that they may trigger some new thinking for you. If you've decided that you want to work on improving your mental health, trying even one of these suggestions can have an enormous effect on how you feel and act:

- Realize that it's okay not to be perfectly mentally healthy and that it's okay to admit to yourself that you have some problems.
- Talk to someone about your strengths and weaknesses—a pastor, counselor, coach, friend, maybe even your partner. Tell him or her you're reading this book and that you want to talk about some things that you've been thinking about.
- Ask people you trust what they think about the status of your mental health.
- Make an action plan to improve your mental health. For example, if you realize you drink too much, go to Alcoholics Anonymous. If you're depressed, frequently angry, or dwell on things too much, make an appointment with a counselor, physician, or psy-

chiatrist to consider the possibility of a supervised treatment plan.

- Figure out what aspects of your mental health have a detrimental effect on your relationship and what small step you can take to change the outcome. If you're like Stan and tend to withdraw, or if your partner complains that you don't talk to her enough or that you never say anything positive, discipline yourself to think of something that's happened each day that you can share with her. If your partner complains that you never think of anyone but yourself, get out your calendar and make a plan for times you'll do something special for her. (Examples: Sunday, May 9—take the kids out for the afternoon; Saturday, May 22—surprise dinner date.)

Build your partner's self-esteem

Your goal is to make the woman in your life feel good about herself. In the past, you've probably tried to gut her self-esteem. Both consciously and unconsciously, you made her feel stupid, and you criticized her because you thought it would make you top dog, increasing the likelihood that you'd get what you wanted. But it didn't work, did it? The truth is that mostly you've been miserable, and you haven't found the caring relationship that you crave.

You need to make a 180-degree turn. Not just a few degrees, but a whole new way of way of relating to her. Instead of telling her the meat loaf is overcooked, thank her for making dinner. If she comments that it's dry, tell her it was fine. Instead of reminding her that her old college friends are a bunch of losers, you tell her it's cool that they've stayed in contact so long. You may say, yeah, but I don't want to lie. But think about it: while it's true that the meat loaf is overcooked, it's equally true that it's good enough to eat and that she *did* make dinner tonight. And although none of her friends is president of Chase Manhattan, you grudgingly admire what loyal friends they've been—in fact, you may be jealous of their intimacy. You make a choice of what you're going to comment on, and you choose to say things that make her feel good and leave out those that will lower her self-esteem. If she feels good, she'll likely feel good about you.

The five-to-one ratio

In a study of couples' interactions, researchers analyzed videotapes of partners in counseling sessions. They classified the behaviors of the couples as either positive or negative interactions. Negative interactions included yelling, ignoring, making poor eye contact, put-downs, name calling, sarcasm, interrupting, and bringing up the past in a negative way. Positive interactions included compliments, active listening, empathy, affirmation, and good eye contact.

The researchers also monitored behaviors of the couples outside of counseling. They tracked how often the couples argued, went out on dates, gave each other the silent treatment, bought each other little gifts, and were supportive of each other. They observed these couples over a number of years and noted how many stayed together and how many got divorced.

Their research showed that couples needed to have five times more positive than negative interactions in order to maintain a relationship. If they had fewer than five times as many positive interactions, there was a good probability that they would divorce. (See John Gottman, "Why Marriages Fail," in *Family Therapy Networker* 18:3, May/June 1994.) The moral of the story is this: stopping abusive behavior is the start, not the conclusion, of improving your relationship. The little things you do, or don't do, count. If you want your relationship to work, you need to engage in loving behaviors. It can make all the difference.

You didn't marry your mother

You are a product of your past relationships, particularly those with your parents, and, when you get in a relationship, you often do not see your partner for who she really is. You see her through the filter of your previous experience, super-imposing an image of your mother (or someone else, such as a former partner) on her. This is called *projective identification*. When you make these projections, you distort your partner's behavior. You can't see clearly what Grace is doing today if you are reacting to what Janet did five years ago. The fact that you're probably unaware of your projections makes them all the more dangerous.

Remember our friend Paul, whose mother was an alcoholic and who was so easily hurt when he thought his wife, Heather, didn't give him enough attention (chapter 3, "Five Lies That Ruin Lives")? Imagine that Paul and Heather are driving somewhere, and Heather is quiet for quite a while. He makes several attempts to strike up a conversation, but she is tired and lost in her own thoughts. What Paul experiences is not a loving partner enjoying a few moments of solitude. He recalls the silence of his alcoholic mother—lost, vacant, passed out. Suddenly Paul yells at Heather, "Why can't you ever talk?" In fact, Heather is usually talkative and responsive, but Paul's hypersensitivity blocks him from accepting the normal ebbs and flows in her behavior. He needs her to be constantly emotionally available to him. When she isn't, Paul's reservoir of trauma and pain and sadness is disturbed. His hurt and rejection from his unavailable mother distort his vision, and he sees Heather as another woman who doesn't care about him.

Another example: Let's suppose you had a former partner, Agnes, who cheated on you. Your partner, Leticia, has asked you to pick her up after work. As you drive up, you see her talking with another man, smiling, and standing, it seems to you, too close. It would be easy for you to project the hurt and jealousy left over from Agnes onto Leticia and see a mild flirtation, or merely an after-work conversation, as the beginning of an affair.

If you recognize that the real problem is the hurt and fear that you project on your partner rather than your partner herself, you can realize that you must work on your own issues. You can watch yourself with vigilance, and when you find yourself projecting someone else's behavior onto your partner, talk to yourself: "Heather is not my mother. I don't have to get upset because she doesn't always hug me." "Leticia is not Agnes. Agnes cheated on me, but that doesn't mean Leticia will, too. In fact, I have no real reason to think Leticia is cheating on me."

Stop dancing

When your relationship is strained, you often think that your partner is the source of your problems. Sometimes it's both of you together. Your pattern of interactions as a couple can create a chasm in your relationship. Chances are that you engage in a destructive dance, maybe even on a daily basis. You waltz around the room, each acting out deep old fears, each triggering the other's deep old fears. This is Jane and Bob's dance.

— Jane comes home and starts to tell Bob about her day at work.
— Bob is preoccupied with his own day, and he doesn't act very interested. He fails to make eye contact, and he doesn't comment on what she's said.
— Jane starts to talk louder, faster, and in more detail to try to tell her story so he'll listen.
— Hearing her demanding tone, Bob withdraws even more.

— Jane sees Bob growing more distant and thinks he doesn't care about her; she becomes angry and accuses him of being inattentive and selfish.

— Bob shuts down completely in response to her anger, throws up his hands in disgust, and walks out of the room.

— Jane starts to cry and yells, "Why in hell did I ever marry you?"

— As he starts down the stairs to the basement, Bob shouts, "You are impossible. You're ridiculous. What a bunch of crap!"

This is not an enjoyable dance. She wants to communicate; he pulls back, leading her to become more assertive. He creates greater emotional distance, and when Jane reacts, Bob takes another step, emotionally shutting down and physically exiting. Jane feels abandoned and brings the whole relationship into question.

When you recognize your steps in the dance, you can catch yourself and stop dancing. But like everything else in relationships, this takes effort and practice. It's hard to learn a new waltz in which you step together if you've been rockin' off the walls and stepping on each other's toes for a long time. You need to stop and look at your partner and give her time to talk without interrupting. Try to summarize what she has said so she knows that you have been listening to her. If you find that one of you is coming on pretty strong and the other person is backing off, STOP. Try to find some common ground without making accusations. It may take two to tango, but it only takes *you* to stop the destructive dance.

Get into reality and stay there

You probably watch too many TV shows and movies that are filled with beautiful and sexy women who talk in low, seductive tones and appear to meet their partner's every desire. Those women are not real, and when you fantasize about them, you know they're not real. There's more danger in comparing your partner to other women, comparisons in which your partner inevitably comes up short.

As an abusive man, you have a record of believing that there's something "wrong" or "not good enough" about your partner. Maybe you wish she'd spend less time at the kids' school and more time with you or cook more and order out less. Perhaps you'd like it if she'd talk less or talk more. Probably you wish she liked sex better and more often. When you dwell on what you see as her shortcomings, you treat her with disdain and even cruelty.

But Eva . . . well, Eva's a different story. Let's say that you have your eyes on Eva at work. She's younger than your partner, Sarah, and more playful. She smiles at you in a way that Sarah never has. She's witty and opinionated, and you love the way she tells off your mutual boss. Your relationship with Sarah seems stale and dreary. You find yourself thinking about Eva when you have sex. You start thinking about leaving Sarah and spending your life with Eva in the Bahamas.

In fact, you know so little about Eva that she might as well be a TV or movie character. You don't know, for example, that she is deeply insecure. She is witty and charming at work as a strategy to get others to like her. You don't know that she has a sharp tongue that can turn ugly, and she and her partner argue most of the time. You don't know that he is Eva's third husband and she's considering leaving him. Chances are you've got it pretty good. But if you let yourself live in a fantasy world with women like Eva, your partner will never stand a chance.

Value what you have and where you are. If you've really worked on your relationship, you have discovered that mature love is based in reality, not fantasy. It's about accepting all of your partner, not just the parts you like. How do you value what you have when your devious mind tells you there's something better over the hill? You stay in reality. You stop your distorted thinking. You say to yourself, "Eva may be cute, but I really don't know anything about her. She would never stick with me the way Sarah has. She doesn't have the steady gaze of a mature woman, and that's what I really want." You stop adding up Sarah's faults so that cheating on her or ending your relationship seems like the smart thing to do, and you remind yourself that you are committed to building a loving, healthy relationship with Sarah. Above all, remind yourself of all her good points. And tell her about them, too.

Dependency

Get some—no, most!—of your needs met elsewhere.

Many abusive men are terribly dependent on women. No one wants to admit it because it's unmanly to be dependent on anyone or anything. But you have needs, plenty of them, and you try to get those needs met through your partner.

Why are men so dependent on women? There are several reasons, but the need to use sex to connect on an emotional as well as a physical level is high on the list. Nature provides men with a bounty of testosterone, a hormone that creates sexual desire, and society teaches men that they can prove their manhood through sexual conquest. But as powerful as the biological sex drive may be, sex is far more than the satisfaction of a physical urge; it's also a vital and often the only outlet for men's emotions. Traditionally, men have three roles: procreating, providing, and protecting. Only one of them, procreating—creating new life—encourages men to feel. The others demand stoicism, fortitude, competitiveness, and self-denial. So, many men use only one means—sex— to express their emotionality, making their desire for sex and the emotional connection associated with sex all the more intense.

Many men tell us that the only time they feel a deep emotional connection in their lives is when they make love with their partners. Most of them feel cut off from people, and as a result they see few opportunities to connect with others, even their partner. Sex creates an instant bond: for a few passionate moments they feel united with another person, body and soul. For many of them, sex is an almost spiritual experience. These men see it as a rare opportunity to feel truly alive and connected with something outside themselves.

Too often, men choose sexual contact at the expense of physical affection: cuddling on the couch turns into sex all too quickly, despite the benefits of a less direct and more communicative form of contact. Our culture offers men limited opportunities for physical contact outside of the primary relationship. Men tend to hold and cuddle their young children less than women do, mainly because women are assigned the primary nurturing role. They may be wary of touching their adolescent daughters for fear of becoming sexually aroused, and they're unsure of how to show affection for their sons because affection between men isn't manly; the fear of homosexuality holds them back.

Touching an adult woman outside of the bonds of a relationship is also restricted because physical contact might be interpreted as a sexual advance or, in the workplace, could be grounds for a sexual harassment suit. Finally, touching a male friend is highly risky because it might be seen as an indication of homosexuality.

Starved for healthy bodily contact and encouraged by society to stay in the box of male socialization, it's not surprising that men demand that their partners meet all their sexual, physical, and emotional dependency needs. Asking one person to meet them all is like driving an SUV around on a kid's bicycle tire: the tire will explode, and that SUV won't get far. Churches and organizations such as Alcoholics Anonymous offer men opportunities to let down their guard, and some men have family members who provide solace. But for many men there are few places outside the home where they feel safe enough to open up emotionally. While your partner may appreciate your trust in her, she will carry a heavy burden if you expect her to take care of all your emotional needs.

In our intake assessments, we ask men who they talk to about their problems. They often answer, "My wife" or "My girlfriend," and then they add, "She's my best friend." Frankly, that makes us nervous. While we think it's a nice sentiment that members of a couple should be each other's best friend, it in fact places too much pressure on the other partner and the relationship. We encourage you to find some other outlets for your dependency needs.

What can you do to be less dependent on your partner? Here are three suggestions.

1. *Take the risk of getting to know some men.* If you give it some thought, you probably know at least one man who will be open to your extended hand. You don't need to spill your guts over a business lunch. By getting to know a man, we mean that you offer him some insight into your own problems and listen attentively if he offers any personal comments about himself. You may even seek out a relationship with someone you admire or see as a role model or potential mentor. If your conversation turns into a complaint session about your partners, then you are not getting to know him— you are only continuing to think about your partner in a controlling way.

2. *Find a group where you feel at home and where you can talk about your personal life.* Maybe you're presented with an opportunity to talk about your fears in a men's study group where you worship. Perhaps you choose "opening up to other people" as the topic for an Alcoholics Anonymous meeting. If you participate in a domestic abuse group, listen carefully to the other men's stories and be honest and open when it is your turn to talk.

3. *Meet more of your own needs.* If you come home from work and settle in for an evening of *Monday Night Football* or video games, you probably aren't meeting your needs for meaning or purpose in your life. Try to meet some of your needs by looking outside yourself. Volunteer. Use your carpentry skills at Habitat for Humanity. Become a Big Brother. Wash dishes at the soup kitchen. Why? Because helping others gives your life purpose, and having purpose in your life makes you less emotionally dependent on your partner.

Fair fighting

Partners in loving, healthy relationships don't always agree, but when they do argue, they do so with respect and empathy. If one hurts the other, they both feel the pain. As an abusive man, you are at risk of trampling your partner's right to disagree or argue with you by using abuse tactics to control and punish her. *The most important step in learning to fight fair is to stop all abuse tactics.* Second, you must commit yourself to the truth that *your right and your partner's right to disagree or argue are completely equal.* You have the choice of fighting in a way that solves problems or continuing to use abuse to control your partner. These guidelines will help you make the right choice.

1. *Find "good" times to argue.* People usually pick the worst times to talk about important issues: in the middle of a crisis when they're both angry and upset. Imagine having a discussion about who should repair your roof—your brother-in-law or a contractor—at two o'clock in the morning after you've both been dripped on for three hours.

2. *Don't bring up the past to avoid the present conflict.* Dragging in your partner's past failures is a cheap and obvious tactic to sidestep the real problem you are facing *now*. Stay in the present moment.

3. *HALT.* Don't talk about important issues when either of you is Hungry, Angry, Liquored up, or Tired. You'll probably agree that arguing when you're drunk or using other drugs is not a good idea. And having a discussion escalate into a war when you're tired is not unusual. The axiom "Never go to bed angry" misses the point. If you can't resolve a problem at midnight, you're less likely to do so with every passing minute. Nothing will be clearer at 2:00 a.m., because there is an inverse relationship between problem solving and how long you've been talking about something. If you find your anger mounting and you realize you are reaching your exit point, take a time-out (see chapter 2).

Choices

Making the best choices now won't necessarily overcome the effects of your bad choices in the past. Working on improving yourself doesn't mean that fixing your relationship is within your power. Your partner has a painful residue of hurt and neglect from your abuse that she may not be able or willing to overcome—at least not overnight. You have violated her confidence in you, and it's no small matter to rebuild trust. If she is still willing to be in a relationship with you, remember that she will heal on her own timetable. Trying to hurry the process along will only mean that you are still trying to control her. In the same way, if you demand that she respond positively to your efforts to create a loving relationship, you will again be trying to control her. Do the best you can to change yourself and to improve your relationship, always remembering that *that is all you can do.* If she chooses to leave, your work will not be in vain. You will have improved the quality of your own life, and you will be more ready to start a new relationship that will not be under the shadow of abuse.

Alcoholics Anonymous members talk about doing *the next right thing.* You can ask yourself, "What's the next right thing that I can do to deepen my relationship with my partner?" Life is really only a series of moments, and those moments bring choices. Picture Conrad (the "Put That Away" personality) walking in the door to find the house a mess. He has a choice. He can complain about the clutter and shout and slam his fist on the table and ruin the evening, or he can take Stacy in his arms, tell her he loves her, and *start putting things away.* He has a choice. *You* have a choice, and on the most fundamental level, it's the choice to be happy or miserable.

chapter eleven

Steps to Recovery

M any men achieve balance in their lives. They meet their needs for companionship and intimacy in healthy relationships with their partners, family, and friends. They also find satisfaction in doing things on their own: they have rewarding work and interests that keep them busy in their spare time. They look to friends and family as partners on the journey of life, but in a personal crisis they can care for themselves without necessarily wanting and needing solace from others.

In contrast, some men try to get other people to meet their needs. They have trouble creating security and happiness on their own. They don't know how to make themselves feel emotionally safe, comfortable, and at ease. They believe, sometimes unconsciously, that others, particularly their partners, are responsible for doing the work of propping them up. Some of these men want to be the center of attention; some want to be served and pampered; others want constant reassurance. When their wives or girlfriends don't meet their expectations, these men resort to control and abuse by demanding, threatening, and manipulating their partners to ease their core fears and make them feel better about themselves. After a while, their demands become habitual, and these men derive a sense of well-being

161

from controlling their partners. Control becomes a way of life.

Addiction

Here is a description of a man who uses power over others to get his needs met:

> He . . . is like an actor who wants to run the whole show; he is forever trying to arrange the lights, the ballet, scenery and the rest of the players his own way. If his arrangements would always stay put, if people would only do as he wished, the show would be great.
>
> What usually happens? The show doesn't come off very well. He begins to think life doesn't treat him right. He decides to exert himself more. . . . Still the play does not suit him. . . . Admitting that he may somewhat be at fault, he is sure that other people are more to blame. He becomes angry, and indignant, and self pitying.

What you have read here was not intended as a description of a controlling man. It's Bill W.'s portrayal of an alcoholic from the "Big Book," *Alcoholics Anonymous*. The founder of AA is describing an addict, and even if you don't drink or use drugs, you probably fit his description quite closely. As someone who relies heavily on control tactics to get what you want, you run the risk of being addicted to control and abuse. There have been times in your relationship when you've thought, and may still think, that if your partner "would only do as [you] wished, the show would be great."

Like other addictions—whether alcohol, drugs, sex, or gambling—your experience controlling your partner offers quick and immediate benefits. Your problems appear to go away and you feel on top of the world. When you lord it over her, life seems to get better instantaneously.

- You get your way.
- You feel powerful.
- You avoid doing what you don't want to do.
- Your partner does more of what you want and less of what you don't want.
- You create bonds with other men, especially your sons, at the expense of women.
- You win arguments.
- You avoid uncomfortable feelings such as anxiety and shame.
- You shut down negative feedback.

Sounds pretty good, doesn't it?

The truth? Your control tactics make your life—not to mention hers—worse, much worse. Suppose you tell your partner that she *will* stay home because you're afraid that if she goes out she'll meet someone else. If you dictate her coming and going, she's in fact that much more likely to leave you: no one wants to be trapped in her own home. But like an addict, you deny, or refuse to see, the truth. You may be consciously aware that you're afraid of competition from other men, but you probably don't know how the core fear of abandonment encourages you to control. All you know is that you want your own way, and you'll do whatever it takes to make her stay home. If you've been controlling long enough and hard enough, your addiction takes over.

The Addictive Pattern

Life for the family of an addict revolves around his addictive behavior. At home, the partner and kids of an alcoholic spend a lot of time wondering and worrying. How am I going to please him? How can I avoid his anger and punishment? Will he embarrass me again? In the same way, life at your house centers on your controlling behavior. Your partner is often afraid and angry about what you have done or may do.

Surprisingly, afraid and angry as your partner is, she will slowly build an immunity to your abuse and control. As a result, you step up the level of your abuse to maintain the control you want. *The addictive process is inherently progressive.* Just like the alcoholic who needs to drink greater quantities to find the high he so desperately seeks, you will be drawn to use stronger and more frequent abuse tactics to get your partner to comply. Perhaps you used to be able to get her to stay home simply by yelling at her. Over time, you supplement the yelling with intimidating gestures: you jump up and move toward her quickly, crowding her until she has to back up. You block her access to the door; you take her car keys away. One day, you hit her to prevent her from leaving.

Addiction, like control, provides addicts with *a false sense of power, security, and love.* For example, drinking can seem like a great idea when an alcoholic leaves work feeling angry about something his boss said. He may feel better for a short time. He'll prop up his self-esteem by talking about what a scumbag his boss really is, and he'll enjoy the support of others in the bar. But the hangover the next morning or the remorse for saying something that hurt a friend or getting into a pushing match with somebody he didn't even know will overshadow the moments of relief he felt the night before. Worse, he may not even remember what he did.

Just as getting drunk may seem like a good idea at the time, you may intimidate your partner into participating in a sexual activity that makes her uncomfortable. At first, this seems like a reasonable way to get your needs met. But there's a major problem. Addictive behavior always results in getting the opposite of what you really want. Just as the alcoholic doesn't improve his relationship with his boss by going out and drinking, you won't encourage your partner to have sex with you voluntarily. She will be less likely to want any form of intimacy, and the sexual abuse will only push her farther away from wanting to be with you or to please you.

Finally, addicts commonly use the cover-up tactics of *denial, blame, minimization,* and *justification* that form part of the cycle of domestic abuse (see chapter 5). Just as the addict will try to deflect attention from his addiction and the damage it causes, the controlling man tries to conceal the seriousness of his abuse from himself and others. "Well, I had a couple of beers," the alcoholic will say, when in fact he drank a twelve-pack. "I don't drink more than anybody else!" The controlling man says, "Everybody has arguments!" when he's yelled at his partner for an hour. He tells his neighbor, "I'd never hit a woman" after he's pushed his partner hard enough that she scraped her leg when she fell down. Even though your partner is less likely to do what you want when you abuse her, as an addict you get what you want *often enough* to continue the behavior. You pull the lever on the slot machine one more time, thinking that this time the coins of power and control will fall into your waiting hand.

Recovering

Addicts are never cured. AA members say they are "in recovery" because they recognize and accept that relapse is just around the corner. One drink is all it takes. It would be wonderful to simply utter a few magic words and have something bad stop and never happen again. We all know that's not the way the world works, and many of us know from painful experience how difficult it can be to stop drinking or using drugs or gambling. Since magic won't work, you need to stage a carefully considered, full-scale attack, mounting all the instruments of offense at your command. AA offers one program of recovery and relapse prevention that has been successful for millions of people. Some of its steps include

- acknowledging you have a problem and asking for help
- clearly identifying the harm done to others and the costs to their lives
- attending AA regularly
- getting a sponsor
- developing a deeper spiritual life
- developing insight into your problem and how it affects you as well as others
- finding new and positive ways to use your time
- avoiding people who use alcohol and places they frequent
- developing a relapse prevention plan

We've adapted these steps in the section that follows ("Relapse Prevention") to help you loosen the grip that control has on your behavior.

Take Stan's behavior on his birthday. He is separated from his wife, Erica. Usually he picks the kids up on Wednesdays. Since it is his birthday, he decides not to pick up the kids as planned but to wait and see if Erica will call him, remember his birthday, and thus give him confirmation that she still thinks about and cares for him. Wanting a "Happy birthday" doesn't seem like much of an offense, does it? But Stan has slipped into controlling behavior (not picking up the kids to provoke a response from Erica) to get what he wants. In fact, he is willing to create disappointment and worry in the whole family and sacrifice his children's trust that Dad will show up on time.

Although recovering from the need to control your partner has many similarities to recovering from addictions to alcohol, gambling, or drugs, there are a few significant differences. First, if the recovering alcoholic or drug addict begins using again, his relapse should be brilliantly clear to him. Although relapse begins long before the first drink (or hit or placing a bet), there is clearly a line of demarcation between use and nonuse. But relapsing into abuse and control is not so clear-cut. Joe is attending a domestic violence treatment group, and over the course of the twenty-six weeks he has committed himself to avoiding abusive and controlling behavior. A few weeks out, he believes his wife paid too much for a new coffeemaker, and he criticizes her for not comparison shopping. A week later, she tells their son he can go camping with neighbors without consulting Joe, and Joe angrily and loudly tells her she should have checked with him first. A month later, he pushes her back down on the couch when she says she wants to leave.

At what point does Joe cross the line into abuse? What constitutes a relapse? If you've been controlling and abusive, you face a stiff challenge: you need to watch yourself and your behavior with the vigilance of a sentry looking out for enemy patrols. All addictions are sneaky and they'll trick you into relapse when you're not paying attention, but domestic abuse is particularly devious because there's no clear mark that says you're abusive or not.

Second, there are treatment plans and support groups for different kinds of addicts. Alcoholics Anonymous and Gamblers Anonymous are well-known organizations where the drinker or gambler can find allies in his struggle against addiction. As a controlling man, however, you're pretty much on your own, because there are few identified support groups. Court-mandated batterer intervention programs are available in many states, but they rarely offer treatment plans that will help their clients to stay clean from control. In chapter 13 we offer you some suggestions on how and where to go for help. In the meantime, we urge you to develop your own relapse prevention plan.

Relapse Prevention

If you were picked up for drunk driving a couple of times, whether in Nome, Alaska, or Key West, Florida, you'd be required to attend a substance abuse group. In that group you'd develop a relapse prevention plan, a personalized program to help you avoid drinking again. Relapse into controlling and abusive behavior is an ever-present possibility in that small moment when you're not on guard. Your goal is to develop a plan that helps you identify, address, and manage your temptation to control or abuse your partner. We hope you take on this problem with the guts and wisdom of those who have broken free of other addictions.

The following relapse prevention program is similar to the Twelve Step model of AA. The plan starts with general, large life changes and ends with small, specific emergency tactics to avoid relapse. Think about each item in the program and ask yourself these two questions for each one.

- Will doing the activity described in this item help me in my war to wean myself from my controlling behavior?
- Am I willing to commit myself to doing it?

If you can honestly answer yes to both questions, then check the suggested action and make plans to implement it. For example, a check beside "see a therapist" would require that you begin to compile a list of therapists and their qualifications, choose a therapist, and make an appointment with him.

This relapse prevention plan is not intended to stand alone. We hope it will give you new ideas to think about and new ways to model your behavior. We encourage you to consider all these possibilities and choose the ones that you feel comfortable starting with. To decrease the likelihood of violence and to ensure that you make the best plan, we suggest you share this plan and your ideas about it with a therapist experienced in working with domestic abuse.

Acknowledgment of how controlling behavior has harmed others and me

_____ Write a letter to myself and my partner admitting my behavior (this letter is primarily for you; you will need to decide if giving it to her is the right thing to do).

_____ Attend a domestic abuse treatment group and explain ways I've been controlling and abusive without minimization, justification, denial, or blame.

_____ Confess to a mentor (an older person you trust).

Life change and replacement activities for controlling behavior

_____ Find ways of satisfying my needs so I don't demand too much of my partner (make new friends, find new interests, learn to enjoy being alone).

_____ Make requests with love, respect, and reason rather than making demands with threats and intimidations.

_____ Work with my partner to schedule and hold family meetings that emphasize sharing opinions, negotiation, and compromise.

_____ Put the wants and needs of my partner and children ahead of my own.

_____ See a therapist to explore personal issues and my need to control and abuse; create plans to deal with these needs and issues.

_____ Observe what makes my family happy and secure, and readjust my behavior based on what I learn.

_____ Socialize with people who have positive attitudes, who are working on their personal growth, and who are respectful to women.

_____ Develop relationships with men who are open to discussing feelings and life issues.

Self-awareness

_____ Be aware of my thoughts and make a daily list—write it down!—of times I engage in positive thinking habits and times I use distorted or negative thinking.

_____ Make a log of minimizing, denying, blaming, and self-justifying thoughts, with the goal of decreasing my use of cover-up tactics and consequent abusive behavior.

_____ Observe myself and be more aware of trigger situations and how I react to them.

_____ Keep track of my abusive and controlling behaviors (see chapter 5) and check myself for relapse into destructive behaviors.

_____ Monitor my emotional well-being and mood (am I relaxed, angry, depressed, loving?).

Personal and spiritual growth

_____ Keep a gratitude journal to avoid feeling cheated by the world and my partner in particular. For at least one month, write a minimum of five daily gratitude entries. (Examples: I am grateful for the good conversation I had with my son, getting the car fixed for less than I expected, being able to take a nice walk with my partner to Dairy Whip, that the Red Sox beat the Yankees, that my boss complimented me today).

_____ Initiate or enhance my participation in a spiritual or religious community.

_____ Take time out for walks, meditation, self-affirmation.

_____ Engage in physical exercise at least four times per week.

_____ Practice acceptance of the many things in life that I cannot control.

_____ Practice recognizing feelings (put a yellow sticky note on the dashboard or computer to remind yourself to do a feelings check).

Positive behaviors

_____ Listen to my partner.

_____ Empathize with her worries and concerns.

_____ Identify what makes my partner feel respected and cared about and engage in those activities.

_____ Choose to do what she wants to do and what is important to her.

_____ Volunteer (give something of yourself at the local soup kitchen or your child's school).

Risk reduction

_____ Manage my feelings so I don't project my fear, hurt, or shame onto my partner.

_____ Find and join a support group; if there isn't one where I live, I can start one after completing a domestic abuse treatment group.

_____ Monitor myself for times and situations when I'm at increased risk, for example, when I'm tired or hungry.

_____ Avoid people or situations that lead me to develop negative attitudes.

_____ If I am a substance abuser or have other addictions, develop a separate relapse plan for these addictions.

_____ Stay away from friends and places where violence is celebrated or encouraged.

Emergency plan: Last-minute tactics to avoid controlling or abusive behavior

_____ Take a time-out, following the rules outlined in chapter 2.

_____ Develop a list of reliable friends to call, and don't hesitate to call one of them.

_____ Carry pictures of my partner and/or my children and commit myself to look at them to help me remember my priorities when I am on the verge of destructive behavior that could harm my family.

_____ Think about consequences—especially for my partner, but also for myself.

_____ Affirm myself: "I can be a good man. I don't need to be abusive. I am a better man than that."

AA meetings take place at all times of the day and night, but the most common meeting time is 8:00 in the evening. The content of an AA meeting is up to the group itself, but at 8:02 P.M., no matter where you live, there are hundreds of thousands of people at meetings reciting the Serenity Prayer because it helps them to keep their priorities straight.

> *God grant me the serenity*
> *To accept the things I cannot change,*
> *The courage to change the things I can,*
> *And the wisdom to know the difference.*

If you're controlling and abusive, this is your prayer, too. You can't change her. But you can have the courage and conviction to change yourself. You can have the courage to end your abuse.

chapter twelve

Roadblocks

In our practice, we find again and again that men who are controlling and abusive engage in other addictive behaviors as well. Many are alcoholics, some use drugs, and some do both. Of men arrested for domestic abuse, 50 to 75 percent are intoxicated at the time of their arrest. Other men have less obviously destructive addictions. Under the guise of taking care of their families, some men work twelve to fourteen hours every day and never take a family vacation. Some of our clients are trapped by gambling. Internet addiction, often to online gaming or porn sites, is an increasingly common compulsion. Our guess is that as a man accustomed to abusive control, you engage in a matrix of addictions. Connor tells this story better than we can.

In my case, there was no single incident that precipitated the breakdown of my marriage. It was not a blowout, but rather a slow leak. I enrolled at the Men's Resource Center's Domestic Relationships Program as a last-ditch effort to save my marriage. Initially it could have been considered the repair mode of my abuse cycle on steroids. To give an account of everything that has contributed to the breakdown of my marriage would take a considerable amount of time, and yet my story cannot really be understood outside the context of my entire life. But I will attempt an abbreviated version that touches on the more salient issues.

On October 4, 2004, my wife finally decided she had had enough of my crap, and for her own well-being and that of our children, needed to take an exit. At the time, I was so focused on me, so entrenched in addict thinking and alcoholic behavior, that at first I hardly recognized the importance of her action. I was shocked and stunned. But, as the day wore on, I began reflecting on my life. And, ever so gradually, the realization that I had a serious problem began to dawn in my mind.

At first I became aware that I was a drug addict and alcoholic and that I needed help. I began to realize that throughout my life all of my attempts to quit or control my use had come to naught. That very evening, I could, and did, admit that I was an addict, that my life had indeed become unmanageable, and that I was powerless to do anything about it. I was both humbled and terribly afraid. Was there any hope? Could I actually stop using and stay stopped? I started crying and praying that evening and didn't stop for weeks. I was a mess. The next day I admitted myself into residential treatment out of desperation, in the hope that somebody could help me put myself back together.

This most recent relapse was triggered by a combination of factors, but its most prominent feature was rooted in my spirituality. By late 2003, I was overwhelmed and struggling just to keep my head above water. Pride and self-will kept me from asking for the help I needed. Like the horse boxer in Orwell's *Animal Farm* I thought that everything would be all right if I just worked a little harder, but I was wrong. As anxiety and fear grew within me, I began to work seven days a week, twelve hours a day, and began to neglect my wife, kids, and my own physical, emotional, and spiritual health. I started drinking and drugging more and more. The shame and guilt pushed me deeper and deeper into a pit from which I could not extricate myself. I soon was in a nosedive without hope of pulling out. Since pride kept me from asking for help in a responsible and mature way, I began pleading covertly. I stopped going to church in the hope that someone might notice my absence and reach out to me. I began "hiding" my beer bottles where they could easily be found. But no one came to rescue me from myself. Not even my spiritual shepherd called on me, and my attitude and faith in God and his people degenerated from complacency to indifference and apathy, and finally to resentment, bitterness, anger, and hostility. Once again I was face to face with the insanity of my addiction. I was spiritually, morally, mentally, and emotionally bankrupt. I could not take care of my family, my customers, or myself. I no longer could care about anything except that next drink or drug. I was a walking corpse, an empty shell. I was a puppet whose strings were being pulled by a drug.

My greatest regret to date has been the neglect and emotional abuse of my wife and family. I can honestly say that while I am using I am the most inconsiderate, selfish, insensitive, uncaring, rude, and obnoxious bastard to walk the face of the earth. Although I've had long stretches of clean time when I am a loving, thoughtful, honest, and tender servant, I have over the past two years unquestionably destroyed the love my wife had for me. My disease and my denial, close-mindedness, unwillingness, apathy, and procrastination have alienated me from those I love the most. For over a year I would not come home till the wee hours of the morning. And when I did arrive I would smell like a brewery and dope house. I would lie, deny, minimize, and become defensive with regard to my habit. I cannot believe that I actually cared more for that shit than my wife and kids.

The current status of my marriage is tenuous at best. It could probably be best described as a demilitarized zone, rather than open warfare. Currently there exists a vast gulf of mistrust that serves to hinder our communication and separate us on both major and minor issues. We seem to be unable or unwilling to overlook any offense. We view each other with suspicion and take the slightest comment as a personal attack. Yet at the same time, we both desire God's healing in our lives, marriage, and family. And both of us want to begin to lay a foundation that will not only endure for the rest of our natural lives, but also flourish.

At times, I even now see myself sabotaging this effort toward reconciliation. I realize that I do have a rather powerful personality, and tend to lack both the sensitivity and the patience to nurture our fragile relationship. I need to cultivate gentleness and continue to work on humility. I no longer intentionally attempt to control and manipulate my wife; however, having used these tactics for so long I must remain ever vigilant or I could indiscriminately undo all the progress that has been made. It is definitely a struggle, and while I believe that I have made significant progress, I realize that this is a journey barely begun. I didn't become a control freak in a day; neither will my recovery be achieved overnight. But I claim spiritual progress rather than spiritual perfection and know that God will continue to do for me what I cannot do for myself—if I let him.

Are You an Addict?

As Connor's story so painfully shows, addictions spin toxic webs around the addict's soul and relationships.

Like Connor, you may already know and admit you have an addiction. However, you may have successfully fooled yourself by your use of cover-up techniques. Answering "yes" to any of the questions below is a signal to look past your denial and examine your behavior more deeply.

- Do you sometimes drink too much? Has your partner complained about your drinking?
- Do you try to stop or cut down on your drinking and fail to meet your goals?
- Do your partner and children complain that you work too much?
- Do you intend to bet a couple dollars and end up losing a lot more than the limit you had set?
- Do you surf pornographic sites, wasting time, violating your code of ethics, or putting your relationship in jeopardy?
- Do you use illegal drugs, or legal drugs in ways they are not meant to be used?
- Do you demand that your partner meet your sexual needs, or do you have one-night stands and/or affairs that damage your relationship?
- Are you preoccupied with playing sports or exercising and find yourself restlessly irritable when you can't participate?
- Do you spend too much time in front of the TV watching sports or other programs, time that

should be spent with your partner and/or
children?

- Do you eat more than you need, especially snacks,
  to make yourself feel better?
- Do you play video games when you ought to be
  helping your wife or playing with your children?
- Do you spend hours every day on the Internet?

If you are going to be serious about recovery you will
need to confront your addictions. If you don't, they will continue to confront you by showing up in your life as pain, relapse, isolation, abuse, and depression. Addictions distort
and damage relationships in five major ways.

1. *Addictions supplant those you love.* You ought to look
   forward to seeing you partner and children, but
   instead you're consumed with getting high or with
   a poker game. Your family ought to be central to
   your life, but it gets replaced. Connor relates loving his family, but in the throes of addiction, his
   love for them was supplanted by his love for drugs
   and alcohol. He wasn't raised to be like this; in
   fact, it seemed to surprise him. His addictions
   pushed his wife and children aside. You may experience your loved ones as a barrier to your addiction. Instead of welcoming an invitation by your
   partner to go for a walk in the evening, you see it
   as an obstruction to surfing the Internet alone in
   your home office. Instead of welcoming her suggestion to watch a movie together, you hear the
   invitation as a barrier to having your buddy over
   to smoke a joint in the garage. Addictions become
   paramount, and you ignore the woman you claim
   you love. Your devotion to the addiction itself and
   to coping with the fallout of your addiction takes

time and attention from where it ought to be—on
the relationship.

2. *Your addiction can destroy your family.* If you drink
    or use drugs, you'll frighten your family. You'll
    be undependable and your behavior will be un-
    predictable; your partner and children will be al-
    ways on guard because they'll never know what to
    expect. You may spend money on gambling or
    drugs so there isn't enough money for the mort-
    gage. You embarrass your children because you
    show up drunk at the school play. You are never
    available to chaperon their school activities be-
    cause you insist on working twelve hours a day.
    You make promises to your children you don't
    keep, such as promising your son you'll go to his
    Little League game, but instead stopping to see a
    buddy who's just got in a new stash of weed. Little
    by little, your addiction causes your family to
    disintegrate.

3. *Addictions make you a liar.* Addictions undermine
    the trust and honesty that are essential to a healthy
    relationship. When you drink too much, use
    pornography, or have affairs, your cover-up tactics
    are lies that compromise the bond between you
    and the woman you love. When your partner is
    lied to over and over again, she will likely become
    angry, and eventually disgusted, with your decep-
    tions. This can lead to her eventually acting out
    her anger, with you justifying your own anger
    and abusive behavior as a normal reaction to
    her anger.

4. *You run away from problems.* A healthy couple is
    a problem-solving team: if there's a flood in the
    basement, if one of them gets laid off, or if they
    don't agree about what new house to buy, they

work together to overcome the problem and move on. If you have an addiction, you run away from problems instead of solving them directly. When you get high—on speed or gambling or sex—you move out of reality. You forget about your problems, and, like a gear that's lost its cogs, you spin out of control: nobody can make contact with you. Things don't get done the way they should, and your relationship becomes a broken machine that sometimes works with starts and fits and other times stops altogether.

5. *Addictions create the attitude that destroys.* Addicts get *attitudes* because their addictions lead them to live failed, miserable, out-of-control lives. They take the attitude home, and people dive for cover because they don't know what will come next.

Bob was the most forlorn client who ever came to our office. He'd been picked up for drunk driving for the fifth time, he'd lost his job, his wife had moved out, and he didn't even know where she'd gone with the kids.

John snarled on the way in. He'd been belligerent with the front office staff because he didn't want to give them his Social Security number, and although he was somewhat calmer once he'd sat down in one of our counseling rooms, he still gave off the smell of someone who would be glad to take on anyone who looked at him the wrong way. He'd been referred because he was caught selling marijuana, but he looked anything but mellow.

Bob is depressed and hopeless and sees himself as a loser. John, angry and aggressive, sees the world as the source of his problems. They respond very differently to their addictions, but their attitudes are equally devastating to their lives and those around them.

The bottom line is this: if you have an addiction—whether it's to gambling or drugs or pornography—you cannot have a healthy relationship. If you want to have a healthy relationship, you must give up the addiction. There is no other way. Recovery from abusive and controlling behavior, as you remember, takes work, hard work, and you will never be successful if you are struggling with another addiction. There are many struggles on the road to becoming a responsible man; giving up addictions is one of the most difficult. It is also one of the most important.

chapter thirteen

The Continuing Journey

Ron W.'s story. This is Ron W.'s story in his own words. He began counseling in the spring of 2004.

What brought me to the Men's Resource Center was not just one incident. It had been progressing over the last five to ten years. Maybe even twenty-four years. We were married very young and we never had much time alone. In the last ten years of our marriage I began to dislike my wife, Stella. Maybe she reminded me of myself, I don't know, but I started to control her. I criticized and humiliated her, gradually breaking down her self-confidence. As I continued to control her, I saw the symptoms of my control in my wife—increased drinking, weight gain, and poor housekeeping—that made me feel that I had to control her more, leading me to intimidate and put her down more frequently. My use of drugs did not help matters, either.

Finally, on January 10, Stella came home from an afternoon of shopping with our two sons. My eight-year-old told me that mom was drinking out of a small bottle in her purse that afternoon. Instead of reacting calmly, I was filled with anger and felt that it was time to end her drinking once and for all. Of course, I had been drinking and smoking dope all afternoon. I approached her yelling and began searching her purse for the bottle. When I couldn't find it, I asked her where it was and she wouldn't answer me. I hit her in the jaw. She was on the phone with her girlfriend, who called the police.

Stella said she was leaving with the kids, but I wasn't going to let her take the boys. I pushed her and grabbed her, hard enough to leave black-and-blue marks. The police came and took her and the boys to her mother's house. She put a restraining order on me. I was devastated and decided that I needed help, and I started counseling with Randy. After four weeks she served me with separation papers. It was a blow, a wake-up call.

In the beginning, I was very uncomfortable in the domestic violence treatment group. I tried to hide in the corner and had little to say. But Randy wouldn't let me get away with that, and soon I found myself opening up to the group and Randy's ideas. Randy said that domestic abuse was a choice, that we needed to be responsible for what we did, and that while we may have been taught that men should be dominant, we needed to learn to treat women as equals and with respect. After a few months, I had a whole different view of what men should act like. I also stopped using alcohol and marijuana, and the fog lifted. Stella had the courts remove the restraining order, and though we didn't live together, there were plenty of opportunities for me to work to be more respectful and caring.

Randy's group lasted twenty-six weeks. During the time that I was there, a number of guys came and went, and despite Randy's admonitions that we needed to continue to work on ourselves, many of the guys plainly did not intend to take Randy's advice to continue with counseling, join support groups, and find other ways of maintaining a high level of accountability. I haven't run into many of the guys that I knew from that twenty-six-week group, but I've heard that several of them were physically abusive again.

At Randy's suggestion, I decided to start a support group. We meet once a week to talk about our lives and if we're being accountable and avoiding abusive behavior. Although I coordinate the meetings, the group is entirely voluntary and leaderless. In addition to the participation in the support group, I speak regularly to various audiences about domestic violence. Over the last seven years, I have given over fifty speeches and a number of interviews.

Stella and I are now living together, and while I am certainly not perfect, I am far from the abusive man that I used to be. It's hard work to be a respectful man, but it's worth it. I keep on with the group—I still go every week after all these years—and I do the public speaking because I know that I will never be completely well. I will always need to guard against the abusive side of me.

Ron is a success story. He's clearly worked hard at making himself into an accountable man. But his story closes with a message that's not easy to swallow: *"I know that I will never be completely well. I will always need to guard against the abusive side of me."*

It seems that life should be easier. Why can't you reach a point where you've made enough changes so you can just sit back and relax? But as you have learned, you never fully recover from your need to control your partner. Like the alco-

holic or the gambler or the sex addict who is never permanently *recovered,* you will always be in recovery. Since recovery is a journey rather than a destination, you know you'll
always be traveling.

Esteban D.'s story. It can be difficult work to keep looking
at yourself. Listen to Esteban D. in his own words. He shared
this reflection with the men in his group on his last day.

I have attended this group since April 29—over thirty
weeks. It has taken me that long just to settle down
and hear what is being said here. I have sensed a slow
lowering of my defensive posture just enough to begin
to change my thinking, just enough to have my heart
softened a little, so that I can recognize the vast amount
of damage I have done to my wife, myself, my children,
and other relationships outside of my family.

It is difficult to identify myself as abusive and controlling. I instinctively recoil. I do not care to look at
myself that way. I do not like these group sessions. I
hate the weight that is placed on my shoulders by this
hour and a half each week. I constantly have arguments running through my head to contradict and
counteract what is being said. Sometimes there is so
much noise from these pitched battles that I can't
hear anything else.

I have thought much about this instinctive pulling
away and these counterarguments, and I am convinced that I fear and avoid the very things I need
most to be changed, to be restored. That is where
those arguments come from.

On some days, I think I am the most brokenhearted person on the planet. Here I am again convinced that I must *stay* brokenhearted. Stay with the

pain and heartache and become familiar with it. Not to wallow in self-pity, but to let the pain open up my mind and settle on my heart. I cannot let myself avoid the hurt with alcohol, drugs, a new woman, pornography, or any other diversion. Perhaps only great pain can destroy great pride.

One of the valuable things about being part of this group is that I am lumped in with a bunch of abusers. I hate that. I hate admitting that I have a place in this group. It is hard medicine to leave a jobsite early every Tuesday to go to group counseling. The men I work with every day know where I am going and why.

A second thing I have received here is clear and concise information on what constitutes abusive behavior.

Third, the discipline of just being here every week and hearing the same stuff over and over again is good. It does not allow me to pretend this stuff will just go away because I don't have to think about it.

Throughout much of my time in this group I have looked to the end of twenty-six weeks as being the end. Now it looks like only the end of the first step on a long, very uncomfortable path. I have to think in terms of years rather than weeks or months. At present, I have committed myself to four individual hours with Randy over a four-week time period. I will continue on after that, I suppose.

Esteban did follow through with the four sessions. In fact, he eventually began individual and group psychotherapy with Randy to delve into the pain and grief of his childhood that had been buried by years of abuse, control, pornography, drugs, and anger. This struggle gives his life meaning and purpose because he is learning that when he has the courage to dig deep into his own soul, he is less liable to hurt others deep in their souls.

Help Yourself . . . and Get Help

Invent and use your own global positioning system. This is a simple invention because it shows only two roads. You'll find you're always traveling on one of the two: recovery or relapse. Check your GPS often. If you're on the recovery road, like Ron and Esteban, you're more likely to have a healthy, loving relationship with the woman you love and be less prone to control and abuse. Should you find yourself on the road to relapse, *stop immediately.* You can always turn around. If you're having trouble finding your way back to the recovery road, then stop and ask for directions from people who know the road.

Ask for help. We've mentioned many times that you'll probably need help to stop your abusive behavior and to gain an understanding of your need to control your partner. Yes, we know this isn't an appealing idea. Men don't like to go to counseling. Male socialization teaches that therapy is not manly. "Real" men aren't supposed to need help fixing anything, especially themselves. Counseling is for guys who can't figure life out on their own. Most men don't want to talk about personal issues, and therapy is all about personal disclosure. Men aren't supposed to experience and discuss feelings—"women have feelings, men get tough"—and therapy is about going beyond the head into the heart and soul. Finally, men with a strong need to control others are particularly averse to counseling: when you walk into that office, you have to hand over some of that control to the therapist.

Your continued growth may be dependent on overcoming these obstacles to getting into therapy. You've learned many important things from this book, but it is only a starting point. We urge you to take the risk and seek therapy.

Choosing a Therapist

1. *What gender?* You may be wondering if you should have a male or female therapist. While there are certainly no fixed rules, we believe there are times in people's lives that they can work more effectively with someone of the same gender. A lot of the work that lies ahead is about recreating your masculinity. Men tend to open up and discuss things in the company of men. Hearing other men take a stand against abuse and sexism can make a powerful contribution to your growth. Seeing a woman therapist at this early stage of your work may make it difficult to confront your issues, especially if you confuse the message with the messenger. If you find yourself constantly thinking, for example, that she automatically blames you for the abuse simply because she is a woman and would never understand you, then you may be better off working with a man until you can confront your accountability issues.

2. *What should he be like?* Your therapist should be simultaneously compassionate and confrontational. You need someone who understands you and your struggle to avoid control and to be a better man. At the same time, he should challenge your abusive behavior and actively work with you to develop and implement a plan for change. We recommend a therapist who has a good understanding of what is called "men's work." The essential message in men's work is that men need to connect with their

humanity and community. This movement encourages men to climb out of their constricting boxes and into open, compassionate, and emotionally engaging relationships with both women and men. Men's work activities frequently take place in organized settings such as support groups and all-male retreats. (See "Resources" for contact information for men's work organizations.) We also recommend that your therapist have an appreciation of feminist psychology, which has helped us understand how patriarchy and rigid male training and thinking are oppressive to both women's and men's humanity. *It is essential that you avoid any therapist who simply tries to place you back in the box or your partner back in her place.*

3. *How do I know if this guy is any good?* Find out the background and credentials of the therapist you're thinking of seeing. His office staff or Web site should be able to tell you about his formal education and specialized training. Just as some therapists specialize in working with clients who suffer from alcoholism or divorce, you should see a counselor who specializes in working with men who abuse and control. Ask if a prospective therapist has attended the Domestic Abuse Intervention Program Training (or something similar). If not, at least find a therapist associated with an agency that runs domestic abuse treatment groups.

4. *Can I fire him?* If you see a therapist a few times and you're not sure you can work with him, let him know. Tell him, "This doesn't seem to be working," and explain why. If he provides you with an answer that's helpful and responsive, give him another chance. If not, don't be shy about moving on. You

have the right and deserve to have a therapist who can be helpful. But be careful. Your fear and need to control may impair your judgment about what makes a "good" therapist. You will be tempted to connect with a therapist who will empathize with your pain and confusion, but who won't confront you about how your abuse and control is causing the very thing you're complaining about. For example, it wouldn't be helpful for a therapist to empathize with an alcoholic who has lost his wife and job due to his alcoholism while not confronting his need to stop drinking. Your therapist may be helpful; you just might not like what you hear.

5. ***Group therapy or individual counseling?*** Throughout this book, we've told you about our groups and the men who have participated in them. You may have noticed that we seldom talk about men who are working on the problem of domestic abuse in one-on-one counseling—that's because we seldom do it. Over the years, we've found that men make the most progress on control and abuse issues in groups. There, men have a chance to listen to and learn from each other. Individual counseling can supplement group work, but it shouldn't replace it or precede it. Since your primary goal is to *stop hurting the woman you love,* it makes sense to begin with a domestic abuse intervention group. After you've stopped the abusive behavior and while you're learning to curb your need to control your partner, we recommend that you continue your work with a combination of individual and group psychotherapy. In this part of your journey you can work on the issues raised in chapter 6 ("What Kind of Man Am I?").

There Is Hope

We imagine that you haven't had a good life for a long time. You have abused your partner. If you have accepted responsibility for your abusive behavior, then you haven't felt good about yourself. You may have changed jobs too often. Other addictions may have compounded your problems. You may have had affairs. If you have kids, you may not have been the best father. You haven't wanted to be this way, but somehow you kept doing things you knew were destructive and harmful. All in all, you have hurt other people deeply, and you felt sad, guilty, tired, and hopeless about yourself.

You've read this book—or at least part of it—and that makes us believe there is hope for you. When you were a flagrantly abusive man with little care for anything but your own selfish needs, your life was a confused disaster. But now that you are working on yourself, you have opened up to meaning and purpose in your life. You realize that you have problems, and you've begun the process of becoming a more caring and responsible man. If you use the time-out accountably, if you stop using power and control tactics and watch for your triggers, if you work to create a respectful, loving relationship, if you become the partner and father you know you can be and stay on the road to recovery, you will stop abusing the woman you love. This is a continuing journey that can't be rushed. Your journey will take courage and work, hard work, long work, but it will be worth it. And it's the right thing to do.

Resources

Authors' Web Site

www.menscenter.org
Charlie Donaldson and Randy Flood can be reached
through this site for the Men's Resource Center of West
Michigan.

Other Organizations

Batterer Intervention Services Coalition of Michigan
2627 N. East Street, Lansing, MI 48906
(877) 482-3933 / www.biscmi.org

Community United Against Violence
160 14th Street, San Francisco, CA 94103
(415) 777-5500 / www.cuav.org

Men Stopping Violence
533 W. Howard Avenue, Decatur, GA 30030
(404) 270-9894 / www.menstoppingviolence.org

Men's Network Against Domestic Violence
www.menagainstdv.org

National Domestic Violence Hotline
P.O. Box 161810, Austin, TX 78716
(800) 799-SAFE / www.ndvh.org

National Organization for Men Against Sexism
P.O. Box 455, Louisville, CO 80027
(303) 666-7043 / www.nomas.org

Peace at Home
P.O. Box 51364, Boston, MA 02205
(978) 546-3137 / www.peaceathome.org

White Ribbon Campaign
365 Bloor Street East, Suite 203
Toronto, Ontario, Canada M4W 3L4
(800) 328-2228 / www.whiteribbon.ca

Publications

Alcoholics Anonymous, fourth edition. New York: Alcoholics
    Anonymous World Services, Inc., 2001.

Aronson, Elliot. *Nobody Left to Hate: Teaching Compassion
    After Columbine.* New York: A Worth Publishers Book,
    2000.

Bancroft, Lundy. *Why Does He Do That? Inside the Minds of
    Angry and Controlling Men.* New York: Berkley Publishing
    Group, 2002.

Bilodeau, Lorraine. *The Anger Workbook.* Center City, MN:
    Hazelden, 1992.

Booth, Leo. *When God Becomes a Drug: Breaking the Chains
    of Religious Addiction and Abuse.* Los Angeles: Jeremy P.
    Tarcher, 1991.

Borcherdt, Bill. *You Can Control Your Anger: 21 Ways to Do It.* Sarasota, FL: Professional Resource Press, 2000.

Carnes, Patrick. *Out of the Shadows: Understanding Sexual Addiction.* Center City, MN: Hazelden, 2001.

Dutton, Donald G. *The Abusive Personality: Violence and Control in Intimate Relationships.* New York: Guilford Press, 1998.

Dutton, Donald G. *The Batterer: A Psychological Profile.* New York: Basic Books, 1995.

Forward, Susan, and Joan Torres. *Men Who Hate Women and the Women Who Love Them: When Loving Hurts and You Don't Know Why.* New York: Bantam Books, 2002.

Garbarino, James. *Lost Boys: Why Our Sons Turn Violent and How We Can Save Them.* New York: Anchor Books, 2000.

Gottman, John. "Why Marriages Fail." *Family Therapy Networker* 18:3, May/June 1994.

Hanh, Thich Nhat. *Anger: Wisdom for Cooling the Flames.* New York: Penguin Putnam, 2002.

Hegstrom, Paul. *Angry Men and the Women Who Love Them: Breaking the Cycle of Physical and Emotional Abuse.* Kansas City, MO: Beacon Hill Press of Kansas City, 2004.

Kimmel, Michael S. *The Gendered Society,* second edition. Oxford: Oxford University Press, 2004.

Kindlon, Dan, and Michael Thompson. *Raising Cain: Protecting the Emotional Life of Boys.* New York: Random House, 2000.

Kivel, Paul. *Boys Will Be Men: Raising Our Sons for Courage, Caring, and Community.* Gabriola Island, British Columbia, Canada: New Society Publishers, 1999.

Kivel, Paul. *Men's Work: How to Stop the Violence That Tears Our Lives Apart.* Center City, MN: Hazelden, 1998.

Kottler, Jeffrey A. *Beyond Blame: A New Way of Resolving Conflicts in Relationships.* San Francisco: Jossey-Bass, 1996.

Kupers, Terry A. *Revisioning Men's Lives: Gender, Intimacy, and Power.* New York: Guilford Press, 1993.

Lee, John H. *At My Father's Wedding: Reclaiming Our True Masculinity.* New York: Bantam Books, 1991.

Marx, Jeffrey. *Seasons of Life: A Football Star, a Boy, a Journey to Manhood.* New York: Simon & Schuster, 2004.

Miller, J. Keith. *Compelled to Control: Why Relationships Break Down and What Makes Them Well.* Deerfield Beach, FL: Health Communications, Inc., 1992.

Nay, W. Robert. *Taking Charge of Anger: How to Resolve Conflict, Sustain Relationships, and Express Yourself Without Losing Control.* New York: Guilford Press, 2003.

Pasick, Robert S. *Awakening from the Deep Sleep: A Powerful Guide for Courageous Men.* New York: HarperSanFrancisco, 1992.

Pittman, Frank. *Man Enough: Fathers, Sons, and the Search for Masculinity.* New York: G. P. Putnam's Sons, 1993.

Pollack, William. *Real Boys: Rescuing Our Sons from the Myths of Boyhood.* New York: Owl Books, 1999.

Real, Terrence. *How Can I Get Through To You?* New York: Simon & Schuster, 2002.

Real, Terrence. *I Don't Want to Talk About It: Overcoming the Secret Legacy of Male Depression.* New York: Scribner, 1997.

Rosenberg, Marshall B. *Nonviolent Communication: A Language of Compassion.* Encinitas, CA: PuddleDancer Press, 1999.

Schnarch, David. *Passionate Marriage: Keeping Love and Intimacy Alive in Committed Relationships.* New York: Henry Holt, 1998.

Index

About the Authors

Charlie Donaldson is director of the Men's Resource Center in Holland, Michigan. He has specialized in working with men for twelve years and offers batterer intervention, substance abuse counseling, and men's therapy groups. As an adjunct professor in the School of Social Work at Grand Valley State University in Allendale, Michigan, Charlie specializes in working with male interns focusing on men's issues. He has presented seminars for other therapists on the psychology of men who abuse women, obstacles and approaches to working with men in therapy, risk and lethality issues for batterers, and interventions for angry and assaultive men. Charlie was instrumental in creating the Batterer Intervention Service Coalition of Michigan and the Lakeshore Alliance Against Domestic and Sexual Violence of Ottawa County, Michigan. He is credentialed as a Limited Licensed Psychologist, Licensed Professional Counselor, and Certified Addictions Counselor I, and holds M.A. degrees in English and Counseling Psychology.

Randy Flood is director of the Men's Resource Center at Fountain Hill in Grand Rapids, Michigan. He has provided specialized evaluation and counseling services for men since 1992, including men with domestic abuse issues. Randy is credentialed as a Limited Licensed Psychologist and holds an M.A. in Counseling Psychology. A member and former chair of the Batterer Intervention Services Coalition of Michigan, Randy has also served as a consultant to the State Court Administrator regarding domestic abuse and divorce mediation. Randy provides consultation and training to organizations and workshop participants on domestic abuse, particularly on intervention and treatment of men. He is frequently sought out by the media to educate communities about sex addiction, anti-bullying initiatives in schools, positive coaching, and raising boys in the new millennium. Randy lives with his partner, Stephanie, and two children, Zachary and Anna.

While completing her Ph.D. at the University of Washington, **Elaine Eldridge** worked at the Fred Hutchinson Cancer Research Center, where she collaborated on writing grant proposals and scientific articles. She freelanced in the Scientific Journals Department at the national headquarters of the American Heart Association in Dallas, Texas, for six years. Dr. Eldridge is an adjunct professor in the Department of English at Grand Valley State University in Allendale, Michigan. She lives in East Grand Rapids, Michigan.